Prepare Now!

A Christian Perspective on Preparing for Hard Times

Rev. Timothy Lee Hickman Sr.

This book is dedicated first, to my loving wife Angela who has stuck by me through thick and thin. I thank God that He sent you to me.

Secondly, I would like to dedicate this book to my mother and father. They taught me so much but importantly how being frugal and prepared was a good thing, even before it became popular.

Table of Contents

Introduction

Ice storms, hurricanes, massive layoffs, and economic downturns. It seems that every time we turn on the news we hear of these events happening more often than not. My intentions for this book is not a doom and gloom outlook, but hopefully give you a better than an optimistic point of view and a peace of mind if things go bad. If you remember the old adage about a pessimist and an optimist it is the pessimist that sees the glass half empty while the optimist sees the glass half full. I believe that with the proper attitude and planning the glass can be totally full, why settle for half full. Many will think this will sound like a pipe dream or a "empower" yourself motivational speaker of the 80's and 90's.

There have been many books that have been written with a lot of good information but none that I had found with a Christian perspective. As an ordained Minister of the Gospel of Jesus Christ I felt this void needed to be filled. Many Christians feel that they don't have to prepare or they feel guilty if they do. Both of these avenues of thought are wrong. I feel that we as Christians have become placid and docile. The "pioneer" spirit that made the United States great has been buried in an unmarked grave, but I say it is time we dig it up and live like our ancestors did with the sense God gave us and the values and morals that are needed so badly in today's society.

The television show "Survivor" has just finished its 18th season as of the writing of this book. I am amazed at the lure of these reality shows, especially "Survivor." Americans love to watch this show, but I believe it is not for the surviving in a wilderness part of the show but for the politics and backstabbing. As the economic downturn starts to take shape in America, many are going to have to stop watching reality television and begin to learn how to survive their own reality.

Think of this book as an insurance policy against bad times. And, just like an insurance policy, it isn't worth the paper it is written on if you don't pay your premiums. This book will be totally worthless if you don't put a plan into action to protect you and your family from the bad times coming.

As I said before, and the title states, this has been written with a Christian perspective. I feel that most reading this book are Christians but there will be some that are not. For the ones that do not have a personal relationship with Jesus Christ, I beg you to search your heart now, not later. As Paul said in Philippians,

⁹ Therefore God also has highly exalted Him and given Him the name which is above every name, ¹⁰ that at the name of Jesus every knee should bow, of those in heaven, and of those on earth, and of those under the earth, ¹¹ and *that* every tongue should confess that Jesus Christ *is* Lord, to the glory of God the Father.

Philippians 2:9-11 (NKJV)

The time that you do it is up to you. As Paul said, every knee shall bow and every tongue shall confess, you need to make plans to do it now, not at the Judgment Day. If it is at Judgment Day, it is too late. You are bound for hell by that time. I don't know you, I don't know your problems, but He does, and He wants to be with you as you go through them. You don't have to worry about your salvation ever again. Just call on Jesus.

²¹And it shall come to pass, that whosoever shall call on the name of the Lord shall be saved.

Acts 2:21(KJV)

Notice He didn't say might be saved, He said "Shall" be saved.

I beg you again, don't tarry, make today the day. Just say,

"Lord Jesus, I know that you are the Son of God, and that you died for my sins, and that you rose from the dead and are sitting at the right hand of God hearing my prayer. I am a sinner. Please,

forgive me for my sins. Lord send your Holy Spirit to me to obey
You and do Your will in my life. In Jesus' name I pray. Amen"

Consider the Ant

Many people, usually ones who have been educated beyond their intelligence ask how I as a Christian and Minister can justify a preparedness lifestyle. Many feel that, as Christians we are not suppose to worry about the day. Preparing is not worrying. Let me state that again, preparing is not worrying, it is common sense that has been instilled by God in many animals yet somehow we miss the boat. We see squirrels storing up for winter, we see the bears getting fat in preparation of their hibernation, we see the bees storing honey for the winter season, yet we look at someone who stores up a pantry of food as a paranoid, worry wart, conspiracy believing, backwoods, camouflage-wearing, gun toting, Neanderthal. I believe that is our own misguided concept that has just recently been established in the United States within the last century. If we took a picture of our ancestors a hundred years ago, it would have been a different story. There wasn't refrigeration so many things were stored in a dry state and usually in large quantities. There was no Wal-Mart to run to two and three times a week to get tonight's dinner supplies. There also wasn't a fast food restaurant on every corner for us buy what they mistakenly call food. People were a different breed then. Many cite the Gospel of Matthew chapter 6:24-30.

No man can serve two masters: for either he will hate the one, and love the other; or else he will hold to the one, and despise the other. Ye cannot serve God and mammon. Therefore I say unto you, Take no thought for your life, what ye shall eat, or what ye shall drink; nor yet for your body, what ye shall put on. Is not the life more than meat, and the body than raiment? Behold the fowls of the air: for they sow not, neither do they reap, nor gather into barns; yet your heavenly Father feedeth them. Are ye not much better than they? Which of you by taking thought can add one cubit unto his stature? And why take ye thought for raiment? Consider the lilies of the field, how they grow; they toil not, neither do they spin: And yet I say unto you, That even Solomon in all his glory was not arrayed like one of these. Wherefore, if God so clothe the grass of the field, which today is, and tomorrow is cast into the oven, shall he not much more clothe you, O ye of little faith? Therefore take no thought, saying, What shall we eat? or, What shall we drink? or, Wherewithal shall we be clothed? (For after all these things do the Gentiles seek:) for your heavenly Father knoweth that ye have need of all these things. But seek ye first the kingdom of God, and his righteousness; and all these things shall be added unto you. Take therefore no thought for the morrow: for the morrow shall take thought for the things of itself. Sufficient unto the day is the evil thereof.

Matthew 6:24-34 (KJV)

Notice that God provides for the birds. If God takes care of them, will He not take care of us? Jesus is speaking of worrying. I have met some people who invent things to worry about. In actuality, they worry about worrying too much. What a vicious circle. I am the first to admit that if someone doesn't have a few concerns about the gloomy economic situations we are facing then they are turning a blind eye to reality. The loss of a job, the higher cost of necessities, I could go on and on, but it serves no purpose other than to depress you. Jesus is telling us that God will provide. Now I know some of my counterparts are preaching prosperity, which is neither what Jesus was teaching nor I. Saying that God will provide means exactly that, He will provide your need. Your need might not be a Hummer or a three story McMansion. Many of us have been living a life above our means. In other words, we have been fooling everyone including ourselves that we have to have the newest technology, the newest automobile, or the newest clothes. We have been fooling everyone, including ourselves. Everyone except God. Nothing has caught God by surprise. But, God providing your need also does not mean sitting on your blessed assurance and waiting for manna to drop from heaven. Jesus said behold the birds; behold means to look at, to watch. Have you ever watched the birds of the field? I love to watch the mockingbirds and sparrows in the yard. They are constantly working. Whether they are finding little remnants of grass and string to build a nest or searching for worms and seeds to feed on, they are constantly working. I think one reason that the birds are used for an example is their work ethic. In the Book of Proverbs our Lord lays out some foundational truths for us to live our life by. For many years I have read a chapter from Proverbs each day.

The chapters correspond to the date of the month, so it makes it easy to know what to read.

4 Lazy hands make a man poor,
but diligent hands bring wealth.

He who gathers crops in summer is a wise son,
but he who sleeps during harvest is a disgraceful son.

Proverbs 10:4-5 (KJV)

10 A little sleep, a little slumber,
a little folding of the hands to rest-

11 and poverty will come on you like a bandit
and scarcity like an armed man.

Proverbs 6:10-11 (NIV)

The sluggard's craving will be the death of him,
because his hands refuse to work.

Proverbs 21:25 (NIV)

All hard work brings a profit,
but mere talk leads only to poverty.

Proverbs 14:23 (NIV)

The Lord tells us not to be lazy first then tells us to gather the crops in the summer. That is the harvest time. This means store up for the winter. The analogy could be drawn to today's society that we should store up during economic good times to aid in the bad times. All through Proverbs talks of lazy men and work.

2nd prepare physically

Now you may be wondering how all these verses on work apply to preparing. Without work, there is no way of preparing. We need to view our preparing as work. There are certain tasks that need to be done on a continual basis in order to stay on track with your preparations. From the earning of the funds to purchase certain items to the storage of food, they all require effort. In some ways it is not a bad connotation to be called "bird brained". If we all had the work ethics of the birds, then preps would be an inborn trait and we would all be ready for the bad times.

How can we as Christians justify the storage of food? One reason is that God encourages us to. We just have to look to the book of Genesis and see Joseph's interpretation of the Pharaoh's dream. Now many believe that the Old Testament is outdated and that none of it applies to us under the New Covenant, I strongly disagree with that precept due to the usage of the Old Testament's verses being quoted by Jesus, Paul, Peter, John. If the Old Testament had served its purpose then why was it so relevant to the writers of the New Testament and to Jesus Christ our Lord? Just because God has not revealed the meaning of a Pharaoh's dream to you doesn't mean that you are not suppose to use Joseph's circumstances to your benefit. Let us look to Genesis to see the interpretation of the Pharaoh's dream.

Seven years of great abundance are coming throughout the land of Egypt, but seven years of famine will follow them. Then all the abundance in Egypt will be forgotten, and the famine will ravage the land. The abundance in the land will not be remembered, because the famine that follows it will be so severe. The reason the dream was given to Pharaoh in two forms is that the matter has been firmly decided by God, and God will do it soon. "And now let Pharaoh look for a discerning and wise man and put him in charge of the land of Egypt. Let Pharaoh appoint commissioners over the land to take a fifth of the harvest of Egypt during the seven years of abundance. They should collect all the food of these good years that are coming and store up the grain under the authority of Pharaoh, to be kept in the cities for food. This food should be held in reserve for the country, to be used during the seven years of famine that will come upon Egypt, so that the country may not be ruined by the famine."

Genesis 41:29-36 (NIV)

What does the seven year of plenty represent to us today? Most of us are relatively in the times of plenty. We still have the advantage of being able to go to Wal-Mart or Kroger and buy the food we need for the day, week, or month. How do the times of famine relate to us today? There are countries right now that people are rioting for food. There are children and adults dying of starvation, malnutrition, and the elements right now. According to the Catholic Information Services for Africa in a report in November 2008, over 5 million Kenyans who are starving around the country due to drought, inflation and the disruptive post-election chaos at the start of the year.[1] That is just one report, the

---

[1] Tales of Misery of Kenya's Starving Millions, CISA , Posted: Thu, Nov 27, 2008

majority of the world live on less than $2 a day. According to an article in Time magazine in February of 2008, things are going to get worse.

Rocketing food prices — some of which have more than doubled in two years — have sparked riots in numerous countries recently. Millions are reeling from sticker shock and governments are scrambling to staunch a fast-moving crisis before it spins out of control. From Mexico to Pakistan, protests have turned violent. Rioters tore through three cities in the West African nation of Burkina Faso last month, burning government buildings and looting stores. Days later in Cameroon, a taxi drivers' strike over fuel prices mutated into a massive protest about food prices, leaving around 20 people dead. Similar protests exploded in Senegal and Mauritania late last year. And Indian protesters burned hundreds of food-ration stores in West Bengal last October, accusing the owners of selling government-subsidized food on the lucrative black market. "This is a serious security issue," says Joachim von Braun, director-general of the International Food Policy Research Institute (IFPRI), in Washington.[2]

---

[2] The World's Growing Food-Price Crisis, Vivienne Walt, Time, Feb. 27, 2008

Just this past year, 2008, in New York, on what the retailers call "Black Friday", we saw people stampede over an employee at Wal-Mart for the special buys the store had advertised. Now for just a moment I want you to think of those same people after the last loaf of bread or bag of Doritos. Folks, I am here to tell you that if you don't think that food riots couldn't or wouldn't happen here, you are sadly mistaken. If you have ever witnessed what the stores look like after the media warns of impending doom, such as an ice storm or hurricane, then you will know what I am talking about on a nicer level. On a side note, it always amazed me when the press was at the grocery stores before a storm interviewing the customers buying carts full of products. When you take a closer look in their baskets, the majority of what you see is beer, potato chips, and just plain junk food. Or their cart is stuffed with 5 gallons of milk and 10 loaves of bread that will ruin after a few days without refrigeration. It is a sad state of affairs that the majority of the public just doesn't get it. Also, I have seen on the news when a major hurricane is approaching the area people are running to Lowe's to buy plywood to board up their windows. My question is what did they do with the boards they bought for the storm a month before? Should storm shutters be a standard issue item on houses in a hurricane prone area? We as Christians have a firm duty to take care of our families. Paul told Timothy the same thing.

But if any provide not for his own, and especially for those of his own house, he hath denied the faith, and is worse than an infidel.

1 Timothy 5:8 (KJV)

Many of my brothers and sisters in Christ have a defeatism attitude. They believe as I do that times are going to get bad just as Jesus told us this in Matthew 24.

Nation will rise against nation, and kingdom against kingdom. There will be famines and earthquakes in various places.

Matthew 24:7 (NIV)

We have witnessed many of these already. We can look to Sarajevo and the Bosnian War. From March of 1992 to November 1995, a country where the Olympics took place in 1984 was torn apart by war. The country and the people were devastated. NATO reported that there were over 200,000 casualties and more than a million refugees or exiles. Bosnia showed what was considered a modern culture was capable of. There were numerous reports of pillaging, raping and genocide. That is just one incident that shows how close man is to the brink of barbarian. Then we could look at some of the natural disasters such as the tsunami that hit in the Pacific on the 26th of December 2004. It is estimated that over 250,000 people perished and millions left homeless. Now a little bit closer to home in 2005 when the Gulf Coast was hit with Katrina. Even with sufficient warnings, we as a people didn't heed them. Two days before landfall, President George Bush declared the area a state of emergency. Still approximately 2000

13

Americans lost their lives. Homes were devastated and most stood there waiting for the government to save them. Problem was that the help did not come fast. Why am I listing off all of these catastrophes? To show that with or without warnings, things do happen, and we need not count on assistance from anyone.

Many Christians are defeatists in that if these catastrophes were predicted then there is nothing we can do to stop it. And if there is nothing we can do to stop it then we must endure it. Just as we read about Joseph in Genesis, the famine was predicted but God showed Joseph how to prepare for it and protect not only his family but also the whole nation of Egypt and the neighboring nations from it.

God has given us the warning. He has not revealed it to us in a dream but in His Word.

A prudent man sees danger and takes refuge,
but the simple keep going and suffer for it.

Proverbs 22:3 (NIV)

Go to the ant, you sluggard;
consider its ways and be wise!

It has no commander,
no overseer or ruler,

yet it stores its provisions in summer
and gathers its food at harvest.

Proverbs 6:6-8 (NIV)

14

I don't know how much clearer God can make it. He has instructed us all through His word to prepare for hard times. If we have heeded God's advice and prepared for bad times, we will quench a lot of the worries that could affect our walk with Him. I am not advocating that we put our faith in a bunch of buckets of food, but still trust in Him to take care of us. Remember the birds. Remember the ants. I know that my salvation is set in stone, I was bought for a price, that price was the blood of my Lord Jesus. So, in the eternal outlook, I am covered. I am covered by the blood. But, right now, here on earth, things are rough and are going to get worse. I have taken steps to not be as bad as an infidel, an unbeliever, as my brother Paul put it. Now I want to prepare as many of my brothers and sisters for the times that are at hand.

2

The Wise Stewart

What better place to start this chapter then to quote my Lord Jesus Christ in the Parable of the Talents. I have heard this passage preached many different ways, but I have always taken it about our stewardship of the wealth that our Lord has entrusted with us.

Again, it will be like a man going on a journey, which called his servants and entrusted his property to them. 15 To one he gave five talents of money, to another two talents, and to another one talent, each according to his ability. Then he went on his journey.

Matthew 25:14-15 (NIV)

Now the first thing to see in the parable is that the Lord is talking about a tangible item, a talent. A talent was not a coin in Jesus' time but a weight measurement. The talent equaled 10,000 denarii. And we can see in the parable of the workers, (Matthew 20:2) that a denarii was considered a fair wage for a day's work. Now if we earned $15 per hour for 8 hours that would equal $120 per day. Then we would multiply $120 x 10,000 so that means a talent in today's amount would be $1,200,000.00. So the sum that the man gave each of his servants was a substantial amount. Notice that the master knew what he could expect from each of the servants. I believe that God will only give us what He can trust us with. If we have not been faithful stewards in the past, why would He believe, just as the master in the parable, anything would change. We see in the next few verses that the master knew his servants well, but he still gave them a chance by giving each at least a talent.

16The man who had received the five talents went at once and put his money to work and gained five more. 17So also, the one with the two talents gained two more. 18But the man who had received the one talent went off, dug a hole in the ground and hid his master's money.

Matthew 25:16-17 (NIV)

We are to use the resources that God has entrusted us with to the best of our ability. You may ask, why does it matter? It will be very hard for us to keep the great commission that we are given in Matthew 28 if we are first off worried about where our next meal is coming from. Think of the work for the Kingdom you could do if, you are debt-free and could take time off from work to serve. What kind of tithes and gifts could you give to further the Kingdom if you were debt-free? But, if we misuse what resources He has entrusted us with, He tells us what will happen.

19"After a long time the master of those servants returned and settled accounts with them. 20The man who had received the five talents brought the other five. 'Master,' he said, 'you entrusted me with five talents. See, I have gained five more.' 21"His master replied, 'Well done, good and faithful servant! You have been faithful with a few things; I will put you in charge of many things. Come and share your master's happiness!' 22"The man with the two talents also came. 'Master,' he said, 'you entrusted me with two talents; see, I have gained two more.' 23"His master replied, 'Well done, good and faithful servant! You have been faithful with a few things; I will put you in charge of many things. Come and share your master's happiness!' 24"Then the man who had received the one talent came. 'Master,' he said, 'I knew that you are a hard man, harvesting where you have not sown and gathering where you have not scattered seed. 25"So I was afraid and went out and hid your talent in the ground. See, here is what belongs to you.' 26"His master replied, 'You wicked, lazy servant! So you knew that I harvest where I have not sown and gather where I have not scattered seed? 27Well then, you should have put my money on deposit with the bankers, so that when I returned I would have received it back with interest. 28" 'Take the talent from him and give it to the one who has the ten talents. 29For everyone who has will be given more, and he will have an abundance. Whoever does not have, even what he has will be taken from him. 30And throw that worthless servant outside, into the darkness, where there will be weeping and gnashing of teeth.'

Matthew 25:19-30 (NIV)

If you are like me, you have read this parable at least a hundred times. The problem I had is that it took way too long for the meaning to manifest itself to me. Isn't God's Word great! I love it when the Holy Spirit reveals a gem of wisdom that I have overlooked for so long. Like I said before, I had read this at least a hundred times before and then in what I call a "light bulb moment" I got it. I have personally been on a roller-coaster ride with our finances. I had gone from next to nothing in pay in the Army to almost $80,000 in my own business, back down to nothing again. The fault all lay with me. I had put my faith in men, not God. I had put my faith in myself, not God. I realized at that moment that it is very hard to see God when you are always looking at others and your own reflection in the mirror. From that point on, I have made it a priority to keep focused on God and what God wants for me. When it starts to get murky on which way to go, or what decision to make, that is when I refer back to God's instruction.

but those who hope in the LORD
will renew their strength.
They will soar on wings like eagles;
they will run and not grow weary,
they will walk and not be faint.
Isaiah 40:31 (NIV)

Wait for the LORD and keep his way.
He will exalt you to inherit the land;
when the wicked are cut off, you will see it.
Psalms 37:34 (NIV)

If we do not use the resources that God has given us in a like manner that the first two servants did then I promise you that you will be tested.

In the past, being frugal was looked at with a bad connotation. Frugal was associated with cheap. Frugality is not a bad word. Frugality is the ability to manage your resources to the best usage. Basically, frugality is being wise with your money. It has recently become fashionable. Many are starting to become "frugal." I say this tongue in cheek, on one report, I heard just the other morning on one of the Good Morning Shows, one way that people can save money is to order their meals delivered to the house. The hostess of the show commented that it made perfect sense, the money you could save by not driving or taking a cab to the restaurant, and not having to tip. I as probably you would have sat in total disbelief. The first thought that came to mind was, how about cooking for yourself? The general public doesn't have a clue. I am assuming that if you are reading this book, you are above the curve of the general public. Some people call the uninformed or not wanting to be informed crowd sheep. I think this does a discredit to sheep everywhere. I don't think that it is a lack of intelligence on the general public's part more so the lack of caring. The "live in the moment" attitude and don't worry about tomorrow mindset has been slowly eating away at our country like a cancer. It starts small and unnoticeable, then it begins to grow, then it takes over in a hurry. This is very evident with America's addiction to credit cards. We want it now, not later. Many of the younger couples fall in to the trap that they should have a house as big or bigger than their parents, they should have all the finer things in life that their parents and others have, they deserve to take expensive vacations. One of the main problems that lie herein is that the parents have worked their whole life and if they are like my parents, scrimped and saved every dime to be able to afford those luxuries. I remember my Aunt Edie telling me how she would walk to town to deposit a $1 in savings. At the time, I thought a two-mile walk for just a dollar was crazy. Now in my older age, I understand. It was a way of life for the people raised during the Depression. In 1960, the average size house was 1200 square feet. In 1974, the size went up to 1695 square feet. Just in 2004, it was 2349 square feet. Now I could understand it if our families were getting bigger but they are not. In 2004 the average household was 2.6 people in 1974 it was 3.1.[3] We have steadily decreased in family and increased in house size.

Frugality is not only a way of life but also an actual mindset. You will have to develop a mindset that every dime you make has to be used to account for something. A $5000 vacation will net you some real great memories and pictures, but that is it. If you are $25,000 in debt you do not need to be taking a trip, you need to be paying your debt. It is a real simple process, but so often overlooked. During this next chapter, we will take a look at different ways of being frugal. Being frugal will require sacrifices, but the means will justify the end. I know I am stating the obvious, but by not owing anyone anything, surviving the upcoming bad

---

[3] Good Morning America, ABC Network, America's Homes Get Bigger and Better

As the American Family Shrinks, Houses Grow; Dec. 27, 2005

times will be a lot easier. Also, as your debt is being reduced, procuring the necessary items for your family becomes reality.

1st Step – Start a Budget

Budgets can be overwhelming at first. But over time, you will be able to know how much is budgeted, how much has been spent that period, and where you can improve it. But, how do you start it?

Now there are plans and books on the market that tell you to list everything you spend for a month. It is not a bad way to get started, but I see it a little different. Listing the spending at the first will not help pay the bills; it will show some bad habits though. I use the list program as a later step.

List all your basic bills in categories. These include:

1. **House.**
2. **Utilities.**
3. **Transportation.**
4. **Food.**
5. **Unsecured Loans.**
6. **Miscellaneous.**

Housing

Housing is the first priority. The reason I list it first is that it should be your top priority. The experts claim that housing costs should be no more than 28% of household income. I say lets take that a little lower. I believe that it should be at the maximum 25% of net household income. If you make $40,000.00 per year and that is all that you have coming in, you have a gross pay of $3300 per month. Of that, approximately $700 per month will go towards Social Security and Federal income taxes. On a side note, if you are getting an income tax rebate every year you are paying too much tax. I tried to explain this to a fellow many years ago and he grasped the concept but then replied, "This is how I save money." Another instance of throwing pearls to swine. It makes absolutely no sense to allow the government to use your money all year long and then give it back the next year without interest. Why should we give the government an interest free loan? So, if you get a tax refund each year, take the amount that you receive and divide it by your pay period whether it is weekly or biweekly, or monthly. With that total, increase your number of exemptions to reflect that difference each payday. It is like getting a raise. Take the extra and either use it to pay down your debt or put it in an interest bearing account. If you are bringing home $2600, your housing costs should be 25% or $650 per month. I know that $650 per month is not going to get you very much at today's housing costs. But it will show you that you are living beyond your means if your housing costs are upwards of 50 to 60 percent of your income. That is what the vast majorities' percentage is. Then they wonder why they can't make ends meet.

If your housing costs are over 25% then there are some things that you can do, although they may not be what you want to hear.

If you can't afford it, **Move!**

I told you that you might not want to hear what I had to say. If you are paying over 40% then you are in a danger zone. If you own your home, sell it and find one that fits your income. You don't have to have 3000 square feet for four people. Here is another thing to consider, don't worry about what your neighbors or other people think. They are not going to pay your bills if you can't. And remember this is a step to be a better steward of what God has given you. God will reward you, remember the man with five talents.

If you are renting, use the same principle. If your rent is over 25% of your income then find a cheaper place to live.

Another place that you can save some money is to check the rates and deductible on your housing insurance. Some have them set to $100 or $250 deductible. Raising your deductible can greatly decrease your housing insurance. There are many places on the internet that will compare rates and give you the best rate. We changed our carrier and saved over $800 per year with the same coverage. That was over a $60 per month raise.

Utilities

We will use utilities as a broad definition for many things that we have and use today. The first being the electric, gas and water. These should be kept between 5 and 10% of your net. There are ways of cutting them. One of the major electric users of the household is the electric dryer. Most dryers use approximately 5kw of power per hour. If your average cost per kilowatt is $0.10 then that is fifty cents per hour. If you run it for 10 hours per week, that is $5.00 or $20 per month. By using a clothesline, you can save that amount each month. Other things that can reduce your electric bill are setting the thermostat up or down 10 degrees while you are away and also while you are asleep will save you upwards of 20% on your cooling and heating costs. Change out to florescent light bulbs. For the same amount of light as a 100-watt bulb you can use a 23-watt bulb. That is over a 75% savings. Unplug all wall warts, those are the large transformers used on so many chargers and appliances, when not in use. Utilize surge strips on all your 110 appliances; some of these draw power even when they are turned off. Reduce all drafts from windows. Upwards of 25% of heat is drawn from windows at night. A simple way of doing this is by placing heavy blankets over the windows at night. There are many more tips that can save you money on the internet at http://www.energysavers.gov.

Transportation

The cost of our transportation has skyrocketed as fast or even faster than our housing costs. Monthly payments on automobiles rival house notes. One way that the finance companies have tricked us is by increasing the terms of the loans. I have seen where there are six and seven year notes now. I have even heard that there are ten-year notes on some vehicles. With the cost of a vehicle over $50,000, no wonder. This makes absolutely no sense to take that large of a note on an item that has one purpose, to get you from point A to point B. The new car on the lot today is going to be a used car as soon as you drive it off the lot. Kind of puts it all in perspective doesn't it. Try to find a vehicle with low mileage and a good report on the internet. Shop around for the best price, and always remember to haggle. The first thing about a vehicle is that you cannot afford it if it cost more than 10 to 15% of your net income. Back to the 40k a year, that will equal total cost for transportation of $390 maximum. That will include the payment, insurance, fuel, and upkeep. Again, you may be looking at these numbers and say that it can't be done. If you are driving a car that has a payment of $500, you are right it can't be done in your present circumstances. Now we have to change the circumstances. If your vehicle is over the 15% mark, you need to get rid of it. You can drive a cheaper car, again are the people you are worrying about going to pay your bills?

Next, check your insurance rates. You may be paying too much. There are many places on the internet to get quotes on your auto insurance. Also, just like your housing insurance, check on the deductible of your auto insurance. Raising the deductible will consequently lower your insurance premiums.

Maintenance is the next step. If you are going to buy a new car that will fit in the 15% bracket, try and get the longest warranty available. Car repairs have escalated tremendously over the last decade. If your vehicle is out of warranty, try and fix it yourself. I know when I first looked under the hood of mine I was overwhelmed. But many of the auto parts places now have diagnostic computers that they hook up to your car's computer to check the codes and tell you the problem. Also, the internet has a great wealth of information on your vehicle. I have been able to save thousands of dollars by doing the repairs myself, and trust me I am by no means a mechanic. I use to joke and say I was a jack-of-all-trades and master of none.

Food

I will not go into great detail on food costs and ways to reduce it in during this chapter due to the upcoming chapters on food. Although I will go over what the percentage should be. I recommend at least 15%. So back to the 40k example, that would be $390 per month. That includes all food, whether you eat out or fix it yourself. Always shop sales, buy in bulk, and use those coupons. My wonderful wife has gone into a grocery store and purchased over $100 worth of food for less than $40. I have known of some who have saved over 90% on their groceries with coupons. That is frugality at its best. I love the old saying, save the pennies, and the dollars will take care of themselves.

Unsecured Loans

This is the area that in most households needs to be cut back on the most dramatically. Unsecured loans are basically loans that have been taken that have no collateral backing them. Credit cards, signature loans, gas cards all of these fall into that category. Some experts say that upwards of 20% of your net income is acceptable for paying on these loans. This is where I disagree with them whole-heartedly. I say that our goal should be 0% of our income should be devoted to them.

The first thing is that if you are using these each month and not paying them off, you have to get your spending under control because you are living above your means. First, do what I call PLASTIC SURGERY, cut your credit cards up! I know that sounds dramatic, but it is going to take dramatic steps to get on the right path. If you have to buy something, do it the old fashioned way, save for it and pay for it in cash. In my own experience, once I have saved for a period of time, the object that I was saving for lost a lot of its luster, and I didn't buy it.

After the cutting, the paying begins. Start with the smallest first. The reason we start with the lowest first, is that when we will pay it off faster thus giving us momentum and a great morale booster. Once the lowest one is paid off, start on the next one. It may take a while, but the interest that you save by paying them off can be used on preparing your family and also for the advancement of God's kingdom.

Miscellaneous

Miscellaneous covers all the other costs. This would cover the household costs like paper towels, toilet paper, light bulbs, etc. It also would cover clothing costs. Many of the expenses can be greatly reduced. Clothing can be purchased used at great discounts. Paper towels can be totally removed from your budget by using dish clothes. A package of $5 dishtowels can last for years.

The total costs of the miscellaneous items per month should be roughly between 5 and 10% of net income.

2nd Step – Create an Emergency Fund

After setting up your budget, your first priority should be to set up an emergency fund. I suggest that you start with $500. If you have set up your insurance plans on a $500 deductible, you will need this if something happens. This money should be put back in cash, preferably in $20 dollar bills at the house. Buy a good safe or firebox and bolt it to the floor, in a hidden place. Only use this money for emergencies.

Once you have the initial $500 saved, then work on the next $500, again in $20 bills. The reason for the $20 bills is that there may come a time when you will not be able to use your debit card or a $100 bill. My daughter was living in Houston during Ike, luckily her house was spared, but she still had to contend with the mess afterwards. It was over a week before they could use the ATMs in certain areas, and many of the stores would only accept cash. Thankfully, she is her Daddy's girl and had her emergency stash of cash at hand.

3rd Step – Quit Using Your Credit Cards

Sounds simple doesn't it? What do I mean by quit it? I mean first and foremost, quit using credit cards. They are a drain on your finances. It takes approximately 16 years to pay off $1000 on an average credit card paying just the minimum. Many people are using credit cards to purchase consumable items. In other words, they are buying dinners out, groceries, fuel and clothing on credit cards. Don't do it. The first thing, if you are not debt free, is to get your spending under control. I will show in the following chapters that a family of four can eat on less than $200 per week. And that $200 is the high side of the cost. If that same family of four goes out to eat at a fast food joint at least three times a week, their food budget goes out the window. Those three meals will cost at a minimum $60. Working with a menu and a budget, that $60 would have purchased over 7 complete meals for the family. That extra $36 per week equals an extra $1872 in your pocket each year. That is just one instance. Remember if that $1872 was on a credit card, paying a minimum of $41 per month at 14% interest, it would take five years to pay it off and the interest would be an added $696 dollars you would pay.

4th Step – Stop Being a Consumer

The next step is quit being a consumer. There are going to be certain things that I will advise you that you need to purchase, but these will be tangible items that will have added value to life. A plasma television set doesn't add value to life, even if it does have picture that looks like you are really there. One way to stop being a consumer is stop buying new. A good system is to buy only when you have to have it and before you buy it, try and find it used first. The only things I look at buying new would be underwear and shoes sometimes. My wife has found new shoes, still in the box with no wear on the soles for a dollar a pair, clothes with the tags still on them for a quarter each. That is major savings. We constantly visit second hand stores looking for items of clothing and items that we can use on the farm for pennies on the dollar.

1. Shop from Second Hand Stores.

    a. Make a list of sizes, styles, and brands that each of the family needs or wants and keep it with you.

    b. Check and see if the second hand stores have a special day with bigger bargains, savings can be tremendous.

    c. Always haggle. Sometimes you may be surprised how little you can buy it for.

2. Check Internet for Bargains.

    a. Check Craigslist first due to it being local hence no shipping charges.

    b. Next check E-bay. There are some real bargains on the largest auction in the world.

    c. The third stop on the internet highway would be at Amazon. There are used items on there also at a discount.

In my experience, most of the items we have been looking for have been found deeply discounted. Remember every dollar you save helps to go towards the goal of being debt free.

The Wise Steward

It has been commanded of us to be wise stewards of resources. Remember that you don't own a thing, God owns it all, and we are just His property managers. If we do well, He will reward us. If we are foolish, He will chastise us. A good example would be a father and a foolish son. If the father gives the son money all the time and the son constantly blows it, then the wise father will begin to taper back the amount or even cut the flow off to teach the son the value of a dollar. I believe our father is no different. If He continues to bless us and we waste it, whether it is money or time, I believe that He will begin to curtail it to teach us a lesson. God is still in the business of chastisement, just as we chastise our children because we love them, so does He.

Lastly, but the most important of anything that I have written is to pray to God and thank Him for all that you have and all that He will bring to you. Ask Him to give you the knowledge first, then the wisdom to be a better steward. I promise you He will bless you.

3

Before It Hits

You may be asking before what hits. "IT" can be a number of things.

Natural Disasters

- Hurricane
- Tornado
- Flood
- Earthquake

Man-Made Disaster

- Terrorist Attack
- Economic Down Turn

Those are just a few of the catastrophes that could affect the way we live. A good acronym for what we are talking about is TEOTWAWKI. This stands for "The End Of The World As We Know It." Any of the aforementioned events could cause a TEOTWAWKI. The hurricanes on the Gulf Coast in the last few years did it for some; the terrorists' attacks in 2001 caused it for many. The current economic situation is causing it for a lot more at this present time. What we will try and do is discuss what steps we can take to insure that we can survive during these times.

A prudent man sees danger and takes refuge,
but the simple keep going and suffer for it.

Proverbs 22:3 (NIV)

God tells us to take refuge when we see danger, but if we have not made a contingency plan to have a place of refuge, then we are the simple-minded.

Like everything we are discussing in this book, we will take an orderly stair-stepped approach to this to arrive at our goals. We first break it down into short-term and long-term goals.

Short-Term

One major characteristic of a catastrophe is that it has no planned schedule. We may be given an early warning consisting of days like in the case of Hurricane Rita and Katrina, or we may have no warning like a terrorist attack. With the fact in mind that we do not have a crystal ball telling us exactly when something bad will happen, we still have to prepare for it. Basically, hope for the best, but prepare for the worst.

Not knowing the timetable, are you prepared for a major event if you are at work or at the store shopping? Is your wife? Are your kids? Do you have the equipment with you to make it back home? What equipment would you need? These are the questions you should be asking yourself. The answers to these questions are some of the short-term goals we will try to achieve.

Short-term goals are goals are for immediate consideration and can be accomplished fairly easily and inexpensively. With whatever catastrophe falls, the requirements are still pretty basic. We all need food, water, and shelter. Those are the basics of life. Without any of the three, we will not survive for long. Another old cliché but realistic is Fail to Plan is Planning to Fail.

First Step- The Plan

The first goal is to set a family plan to get everybody home. If it is just you or you and your spouse, and you both work in the city, establish a meeting place. Remember, there may not be any communications so it will be too late to try and get hold of each other after the event has taken place. Once you have a meeting place established, have at least three routes established to get back home. Plan on leaving one vehicle there so that you can remain together.

For those with children as we have, the next step of the family plan is to retrieve the children. Our plans, up until one of the kids started driving to school, was for us to make a beeline to the school. One contingency that we had in picking up the children was that we would park a few blocks from the school and walk up to get the kids. We have seen what a madhouse the school is with vehicles and gridlock on a normal day. We can only assume that it will be that plus total mayhem if a major event has occurred. Once the oldest child started driving the plans changed slightly. It was up to the oldest to retrieve the others from the school and drive straight home. If the roads were impassable, they had a BOB (Bug Out Bag) with them and they could walk home. Luckily, the school was just a few miles from the house.

The answers to some of the short-term goals, every vehicle should have a BOB. Now that is not your Uncle Bob, it is an acronym to Bug Out Bag. The BOB is a kit that can be assembled at home and carried in the trunk or under a seat in your vehicle to give yourself a better chance of getting back home. We use a backpack that is U.S. Army issued called an ALICE medium pack. ALICE is another acronym for All-Purpose Lightweight Individual Carrying Equipment. Basically an Army backpack. They can be bought used in good serviceable condition at any Army-Navy Surplus store or on E-bay for around $20 to $30 with frame and straps. There are better backpacks on the market but for the price, you can't beat it for its durability and purpose. The reason we use an ALICE pack over say a book bag or duffle bag is that it will stand up to more wear and it can provide you for hands free carry if you are forced to hike it back home.

The Gear to Store in Pack:

1. Maps of your area. These should include road maps and topographical maps or even satellite photos of all the areas of your route. Remember to have more than one route back home. Your normal route may pass through a bad neighborhood, or cross multiple bridges that may not be there, or they may be so jammed with traffic that they are impassable. Remember what the highways looked like from Houston to Dallas before Rita hit? People sat on the highway for hours. Delorme makes a great set of books call the Gazetteer. They are broken down by state and are highly detailed. The other maps or satellite photos can be acquired on the internet. A good place to look at is http://maps.live.com/ they have satellite and aerial photos of most areas. These can help with obstacles that would cause a problem. Try and get the photos and the maps laminated so that they will be waterproof and will last longer. Place these in the top pocket where they will be easily accessed.

2. Good Quality compass. I prefer the military lensatic compass. This is not a place to skimp and buy a cheapy.

3. A notebook, pencil and pen. Put these in a Ziploc bag also at the top.

4. One set up of outer clothing. I prefer using 511™ or BDU pants and shirts. They are rugged and will hold up. The only problem with camouflage is that it could draw attention to you more so than civilian clothes. Store in waterproof bag.

5. T-shirt and a change of underwear. Also stored in waterproof bag.

6. At least three pairs of socks. Also stored in a waterproof bag.

7. Good set of hiking boots. I prefer Rocky™ brand that are waterproof and also insulated. Always take care of your feet, a lesson I learned in the Army. I still remember all the people crossing the Brooklyn Bridge heading home after the terrorist attacks in New York City. I wondered how many were prepared for that walk. Make sure that the boots have been broken in. A long march home is not the place to break them in.

8. A good military poncho. This can keep you dry as well as double as a shelter. They can be purchased on the internet for under $20.

9. Good set of work gloves. You don't know what kind of debris you may have to move or cross over.

10. Roll of duct tape stored in a Ziploc™ bag. This is the redneck in me, you can fix just about anything with duct tape.

11. A roll of ¼" nylon rope x 100'. This can be used to hold something together or help to rig a shelter with the poncho.

12. A multi-purpose tool. We prefer the Leatherman™ line. These are tools that have pliers, knives, screwdrivers, and on some models, scissors. I can't remember how many different items I have repaired with my Leatherman.™

13. A good quality fixed blade knife with at least a 4" blade. I prefer the ColdSteel™ brand. They are rugged and the sheaths are well made.

14. Food. I carry at least 3 MREs, which is another military acronym for Meals Ready to Eat. These provide approximately 1200 calories. They have a shelf life that is shortened by high or low temperatures. If the BOB is stored in the trunk of a car, the MREs will need to be rotated at least every 6 months. They cost approximately $5 ea.

15. Knife, Fork and Spoon. Eating utensils are provided in the MRE, but I still prefer to carry an extra set.

16. Water. On the outside of the ALICE pack are straps that an Army canteen cover can be affixed to. Buy at least two complete setups of the canteen. This will include the

canteen, the canteen cup, and the canteen cover. This will give you two quarts of water plus the added canteen cup to use to eat, drink and cook with. I have seen these sell for $2 for the whole set up.

17. Potable Aqua tablets. These are tablets used to purify water. They can be purchased at Wal-Mart or from Amazon.com.

18. First Aid Kit. Try and get a good quality, multipurpose one. This will run about $10 to $15 at Wal-Mart.

19. Waterless Hand Cleaner. This also can be purchased at the larger discount centers.

20. Toilet paper. Store this smashed down in a Ziploc™ bag. You will never know the value of this item until you need it.

21. Flashlight. I actually carry two. One is a small "AA" type Maglite™ and the other is a "D" cell Maglite™. I prefer the LED style. Some people I know carry the windup style flashlights. These just do not have the power I like. Another good addition would be some of the new LED headlamps. These have straps that allow you to mount it on your forehead so you can have your hands free. Always make sure you have extra batteries for each.

22. Communications. I carry a small walkie-talkie type CB radio that runs off batteries or car lighter. These types do

not have a lot of range, but it possibly could save your life one day.

23. A couple of small disposable lighters.

24. Prescription eyeglasses if needed.

25. At least a week of prescription drugs.

26. Pain reliever. This could be Acetaminophen or Aspirin, your pick.

27. Gas siphon pump, to possibly use to siphon gas from other vehicles. These can be bought at most auto parts stores like Pep Boys for around $15.

28. Depending on the season, I like to have insulated underwear and a poncho liner during the winter.

With this basic list, you should be able to get home. We have covered the three basic needs, food, water, and shelter. The only other need is one that is a personal preference. That is the need for security. I carry a personal sidearm and at least four spare magazines. In some areas of our country this may also be illegal. It has become a sad part of legislating our rights away. Again, I'll reiterate, all of this is your own personal choice.

I consider everything listed above as a bare minimum. There are other objects that can be placed in your BOB. Take a little time and think about you own scenarios and what would be beneficial to you.

Now that everyone is home safely, first a big sigh of relief and a prayer of thanksgiving to God.

Second Step – The Home

Your house is your shelter but without contingency plans and equipment in place, you may have to leave your home. Take time right now and think what if. What if the power does not work for an extended amount of time, what will you do? What if a major event occurs and family and friends look to you for aid, do you have the room? What if the major event is civil unrest, are you in a "high" risk zone? Or, can you defend your family from others wanting to do you harm? These are just some of the questions that come to mind. Each scenario is different, and there could be a hundred or more different scenarios that could take place. Any form of major event from the loss of job to civil unrest to natural disasters can occur and now is the time to plan for these events, not when they happen. Many of the main events have commonality of some aspects of the solution.

The home is going to either be your Bug Out jumping off point or your Bug In position. Bugging out may not be an option for you depending on the scenario so we plan to Bug In. This means that we will ride out the storm at the house. Now if there is a hurricane coming or the house has been damage by another calamity, this will not hold true. If that is the case, there may not be any supplies left at the house. That is where you will need a Bug Out Location. This could be a relative or friend a distance away from the house or it could be a piece of property that you have acquired that is set up for just such emergencies. If it is with a relative or friend, try to set up storage of some of the items we will be discussing in this chapter due to the fact that you may not be able to drive to them and will not be able to carry it all. If it is another shelter that you own that is away from the home, your gear may not be safe with no one to watch it. A good idea may be to store it in a storage facility between you and the Bug Out Location. This way you could pick it up if you are driving, or if on foot to it you could have another mode of transportation there waiting. The transportation could be a small pickup that you have purchased or as simple as bicycles with buggies on the back. I know that there are a lot of holes in the plan, but again it is all going to depend on your circumstances.

Bugging In is probably going to be what the majority of the population will be doing. The basics that we discussed for the BOB are going to be the same, food, water and shelter. We are going to look at each in detail.

Food

I have two chapters dedicated to the procurement of your food so I am going to briefly discuss the preparations of food in this section. If power has been lost, how will you cook the foods that you have stored? If your stove is electric and you have no power, you have a very expensive cabinet. If you have a natural gas range, you may have gas pumping as long as the pumping stations are still in operation, but you are still dependant on someone else. Our goal will be to become self-reliant. There are many ways to accomplish this.

Propane stove

If you have a range that is run on propane, then you have a tank that is usually 250 to 500 gallons on site. Always have it topped off each month. I have an acquaintance that waits until the last minute, even in winter, to have his filled. This could be a major problem if you are counting on it to heat the house and cook your food. Stay on top of it and read your meter once a week. Soon you will have a good idea of your consumption rate and will be able to forecast when you need it filled. My suggestion is at least once a month top it off.

Camp Stoves

I like the idea of having camp stoves. The reason being is that it is portable and can be used in both Bug Out and Bug In. There are many types on the market. We have incorporated ours with the fuel being able to cross over to our light, cooking and heating. This way we store one fuel for three items versus three different fuel systems. We chose a Coleman™ propane two burner stove. It can be placed on the stove itself or used with the fold up stand that we purchased separately. It can be used with the 1lb. cans or with the 20lb. tanks that are common with the outside grills. There are also bigger tanks on the market but for the ease of storage, filling and exchange we store our fuel in the 20lb. bottles. In order to use the larger tanks with our stove, an adapter hose had to be purchased separately. Try and procure as many of the bottles as possible. I have picked up some on the side of the road when people have thrown out their grill; they left the tank on it. I have also purchased some for as little as $5 each at yard sales. Try and get as many as you can as cheaply as you can and make sure that they are filled. A twenty-pound tank can last for about 50 hours on one burner at medium heat. Needless to say, conservation should be the order to preserve the fuel. We will not know when the power comes back on, and cold food or no food is a serious morale destroyer. Another alternative for fuel is the Coleman Dual Fuel Stove that costs around $50 to $60. This stove uses liquid fuel like Coleman's camp fuel or unleaded gasoline. This way you can utilize the fuel you have stored for your vehicle or generator. One caution is that I would never use this stove inside the house for fear of fire.

Wood Stove

Wood stoves have greatly improved over the last hundred years, but their basic usages are still the same. They require wood to cook with. An insert in a fireplace is not a very good choice. An actual cook stove is what is needed. Most have a flat surface that can be used for the pots and skillets and some have an oven and a water heater on them. The models that are efficient and have the add-ons like oven and water heater are usually the most expensive. They are well worth the money but one draw back is that they take quite a bit of space for the stove and the wood to fuel it. They are not as efficient as the camp stoves either.

Water

Most of us do not realize how much water we use everyday. If your water bill itemizes it, I think you will be shocked. A typical bath uses 36 gallons of water where a shower may use 25 to 50 gallons. The newer showerheads cut the amount of flow down to 2 gallons per minute. If there are four people in the house and they take a 10-minute shower everyday, that is 2400 gallons per month. The old style toilets use approximately 6 gallons of water with every flush. The new conservative toilets only use 1.5 gallons per flush. But if the toilet is flushed 10 times a day, that equals 450 gallons of water per month.

Seeing the amount of water we use normally, conservation is going to be the key to water storage. Some experts suggest at least a gallon per person per day for drinking and cooking. I like to increase this amount to at least 2 gallons per person per day for at least a week. For a family of four that equals 56 gallons. Now this can be stored in numerous ways. One is in 55-gallon plastic drums; another is in 6-gallon water cans that can be purchased at the discount stores. The 6 gallons cans weigh approximately 42 pounds each while the 55-gallon drums will weigh in at 385 pounds. Also the drums will require a pump to get the water out of them. If the water is still working when you return home, fill the bathtub and every item you can think of with clean water. Also, another source of water that is already stored in your house is in your water heater. Depending on the size, you could have 40 to 60 gallons of water stored there.

A water filter is the best thing to use to procure water from sources that might not be reliable. A Berkey water filter is one of the most popular on the market today. These cost from $200 to $300 each and the filters will last from up to 2000 gallons of water. They are a little pricey but well worth the investment.

Boiling is the next best thing that can be done with water if you are not sure of its pureness. Heat the water to a rolling boil and keep it boiling for several minutes. To save fuel, cover the pot.

After boiling, bleach would be our next step. A gallon of common bleach that has no additives like soap, phosphates or fragrance will purify 3800 gallons of water. If there are any particles in the water let it stand for a period of time and the particles will settle. Pour the water into a clean container and add 8 drops of bleach to one gallon of water and mix well. Let it sit for 30 minutes then smell the water. It should have a slight bleach smell if not; add 8 more drops and let sit for 15 minutes. Continue until you have a slight smell. Pour the purified water between clean containers to remove some of the bleach taste.

One solution to the water problem is a well. We have both "city" water and well water. We use the well water to water the garden and livestock but we also have a contingency plan that if the pumping stations quit working, we will switch the house over to well water. Our well is 185 feet deep so it requires a 220v pump. If the power goes out, I have wired the pump so that our generator can run the pump. But, even though we have a pump and way of operating, we still have plans in case we can't use the pump with purifying water collected in the area. Always have a backup plan to a backup plan.

Power

One item that hasn't been covered yet is power. We have become dependant on electricity that we expect the light to come on when we hit the switch. Here is what we need to do when the switch doesn't work.

First we need to list the important items that we will have to have and then look at solutions to solve the problem.

Lighting is the first we will look at. Having light in the house is a comfort if you don't it can be a real burden. There are many ways to have light in the house. The simplest solution is candles. Candles can be bought inexpensively at most discount stores. The drawbacks of using candles for light are that they are not very efficient, they are not renewable, and they have the potential of a fire hazard while in use. With these drawbacks known, they still should be considered as part of your equipment. Always use in a safe manner and keep away from combustible material. Caution should be exercised when used around children; most children have a large fascination with a burning candle. It only takes one mistake to lose your whole house.

Lanterns are the next step from candles. There are many varieties on the market today. I remember growing up there were only the table lamps and camping lanterns. The table lamps were the type used by my grandparents to light the house after dark. Many people know them by the trade name "Aladdin" even though others may have made them. The table lamps use a mantle and kerosene or lamp oil to light by. They can provide up to about 100 lumens. Lumen is the unit that light is measured with. A 100-watt bulb emits approximately 1500 lumen. So with that fact known, we see that a kerosene lamp does not emit much light, but it beats the dark. The drawbacks of the table lamp are that they are not renewable, they are not very efficient, and they also have the potential of a fire hazard. Identical drawbacks to the candles, but still one-step up.

Camping lanterns are where there have been definite improvements over the last fifty years. The types that are available are battery, electric rechargeable, propane, and liquid gas. Of the types listed, we have utilized each one. As with candles and table lamps they each have their own drawbacks. The battery-type lanterns are good for short-term lighting but their drawback is that the larger ones really burn up some batteries. There are some really good LED AA battery lanterns on the market today that emit quite a bit of light and are easy on the batteries. We use a Rock River LED that uses 4 AA batteries. We use rechargeable batteries for the economy. It puts out approximately 5 Lumen and will give you light for about 6 hours before you have to either replace the batteries or recharge them. I like the AA feature due to us using quite a few AAs in our small flashlights and radios that are in our equipment. The larger lanterns that use the D cell batteries downfall is that they burn up the batteries so quickly. Stick to the small ones for using in short time. Using a battery lantern for an extended time is not very efficient. The rechargeable lanterns have about the same drawbacks as the battery style. They are basically the same units with rechargeable battery packs. Major advantage of using battery lanterns is that there is no fire hazard.

The propane lanterns on the market today are very good. The double mantle emits approximately 1000 lumen or the equivalent to 65-watt electric bulb. I prefer the manual lighted models only because it is one less part that can go bad. The lantern can run for about 8 hours on one 1lb. bottle of propane.

The gas model lanterns are also very good. The dual fuel lanterns can use unleaded gasoline or camp stove fuel just like the dual fuel stoves. Try and combine the fuels for your stove and lanterns. We actually have both types. Again, back up of a back up.

One other solution that we use is a DC battery back up system for power. We started using this setup while on road trips to power computers and other equipment but have since started using it during blackouts at the house.

The whole set up is fairly inexpensive but it is worth its weight in gold during the blackouts. In early 2008, we had tornadoes all around our area. Two touched down less than a mile from our house and knocked out power all down the road. After about 5 or 6 hours the utility company repairman knocked on our door to ask how we had power. He commented that he hadn't heard a generator running but saw the lights and television were on. I just grinned and said it was all run on batteries. From the bewildered look on his face he either thought I was crazy or he was going crazy.

Our system starts out with a Type 27 deep cycle battery. We started with a Wal-mart brand Marine battery rated at 105Ah. The 105 Ah is a typical battery size. If you multiply 12 volts (size of battery) x 105Ah = 1260 watt hours. You don't want to discharge the battery over 50% so that equals 630 watt-hours. The one battery will run a set of 4 compact fluorescent lights that are rated at 13 watts for 12 hours. The whole system is one 12v Deep Cycle Battery $70, one inverter $50, and one battery charger $40. All of these items can be purchased at Wal-mart or other discount stores. The battery charger is to keep your batteries topped off when the power is on. An add-on that can be purchased later is a solar panel charger. The small 5-watt types you see at the auto parts places are not sufficient enough to charge your battery. At least 45 watts is needed. The way the panels charge is that 45 watts represents how many watts that the panel will charge at 100% efficiency, which it will never do, per hour. If you average 6 hours of sunlight per day, you are only adding back 270 watts. We just saw that we pulled 630 watts with the light bulbs. But, every little bit helps. The solar panels are currently selling for $5 per watt. The 45-watt should cost around $200.

All the different systems we have looked at previously have just covered the small loads in the house. Let's look at the large loads.

Dishwasher now becomes a sink, soap, and dishrags. Do you have hand dishwashing detergent and hand towels?

Clothes washer now becomes a wash pan, soap, and a scrub board. Do you have a scrub board and wash pan?

Air conditioning now becomes open windows and possibly some small fans run off the battery backup. Are your screens serviceable, think bugs?

All of the appliances that are listed above are actually convenience appliances. Many of what we use today is convenience. Refrigeration is one appliance that is not a simple convenience. Most refrigerator/freezers pull about 400 watts when the compressor kicks in. Only when it is running will it pull that type of wattage. In the winter of 1994 we had a horrific ice storm that knocked our power off for 14 days. That is when we decided to add a generator to our system. Like many of our first attempts to be self-sufficient, our generator purchase was not the best bang for the buck. Hopefully, you will not make the same mistakes we did.

Generators come in different sizes, fuels, and brands. Many run out after a major event and buy the first one they can at the building supply outlets. These are usually not the best choices for your home contingency plans. But, they are starting to carry some major brands. Our first was a 5500-watt manual start. It was loud and very inefficient. It had enough wattage to power what we wanted but it was a killer to get started and you couldn't hear yourself think when it was running. It had no oil filtration system or a governor. Basically it would run full throttle whether you needed 200 watts or the full 5500 watts. Below is a list of features needed for your generator.

1. Efficiency, maximum of ½ gallon of fuel per hour for 4000 watts.
2. Oil filtration system. Oil is the lifeline of the generator.
3. An auto-idle to conserve fuel.
4. Capacity to charge DC.

There are many generators that will fit these requirements. Honda's model EU3000 is a great model but is limited to 3000 watts. But it is one of the most efficient generators on the market. The EU3000 can be run for up to 20 hours on 3.4 gallons of gasoline. The EU3000 is rather expensive though, ranging from $1700 to $2000. The Yamaha EF3000 is also similar in functions and price. A good quality generator is the Generac Model 9777 4000-watt. It had all the features we were looking for plus it was below $1000. It cranks of the first pull, and is very efficient. We can average between three to five hours on one gallon of gasoline powering most of the house except for the central air unit.

Our contingency plan is to run the generator long enough to cycle the refrigerator and freezers, pump enough water from the well to last a day, and charge the batteries in our battery bank. By running the generator every 6 hours for 1 hour at a time, a supply of 20 gallons of fuel will keep the refrigerator and freezer running for approximately 30 days. Basically the food we have in the freezers will be gone before the fuel is. If after 30 days we are still not able to acquire fuel, then we will have a considerable amount of problems to contend with.

Regardless of what generator you decide on, make sure that it has the capabilities we listed earlier with fuel efficiency at the top of the list.

Once you have acquired your generator you now have to decide how to power the house. The safest yet most expensive way to power the house is to add a transfer switch. This unit has to be installed by an electrician. The transfer switch allows you to hook up your generator to the house without back feeding thru the main line. Without the transfer switch, a utility worker could be electrocuted down the line from you by the power produced by your generator. The average cost should run about $200 for the part and another $200 for the installation.

Another way that some power their house is to install a 220v plug, like what a clothes dryer uses, then use a cord made with two male ends so that one end can plug into the generator and the other into the plug. The homeowner shuts off the main breaker in their panel. This cuts the power from going anywhere but into the house circuits.

The last set up is not the best, but is probably the cheapest. The majority of the items you will have running during the blackout will be 110v. With that being said, a couple of good quality extension cords with circuit breaking strips added to them will power everything you need. If necessary, move the essential appliances to one location for ease of running the cords. One thing to remember is that the longer the extension cord the more power that is lost. Also, if you are going to use this setup for power, don't buy the cheap 14ga. extension cords; get at least a 12ga. or 10ga. cord.

The last item to discuss for the house is heat. We can survive in the summer without air conditioning, but without heat you can freeze to death. There are various means to heat the house. First step though is to centralize all operations in the house in a survival situation. This may mean moving mattresses into the largest room and everyone sleeping there. If there were a room with a fireplace, this would be the best location. Needless to say, have enough wood for the winter on site. I have seen the little bundles of what I would consider kindling being sold at grocery and convenience stores for a few dollars. I have asked myself, "Who in the world would buy that little amount of wood?" But, I guess that people do or they wouldn't be selling them. If you have a standard fireplace now is the time to look into a more efficient stove insert or a stove that can be vented out of the fireplace. The $500 investment on the stove will save you money in the long run on heating bills and wood costs even if you never experience a major event.

Regardless of whether you have a fireplace, there are still steps to help the heating of your room. One is to try and find blankets or quilts on the cheap at a second-hand store or discount store. Once you have them, cut them to the size of your doors and windows in the room. Sew the edges so that they will not unravel. Then purchase some Velcro and sew it onto the edges of the blankets. Place the other side of the Velcro on the door or window frame.

If you don't have a fireplace, there are still ways to heat your house. The easiest we have found are the vent-less propane heaters. Remember we discussed earlier trying to economize our fuels by using the same for our lighting, cooking and heating. A vent-less heater can be installed on the wall of the room with hookups for hoses that position the tank on the outside of the house. Always think safety first. Open flames and propane tanks are not a good mix. If the wall mounted vent-less heaters are not an option then the next step is a portable propane heater. There are many types out there, but remember safety. Try and find one that has a safety turn over shutoff. That way if the unit is knocked over it will shut the gas off. One important thing to remember is that if a heater is not designated as a vent-less heater, carbon monoxide is emitted into the heating area along with the heat. It is not recommended that any of the portables be used in a confined space. With that in mind, use at your own risk. Some compensate for the carbon monoxide by opening a window slightly. Kerosene heaters are also another alternative. They are similar to the propane heaters in safety. Remember to always use kerosene and never gasoline in kerosene heaters. Also, let the unit cool and fill the tank outside of the house. Those are the choices for heating the house when the utilities are down. Wood is the only renewable and longest lasting of the three. With propane and kerosene, your heating source is only good as long as your tanks have fuel. If the infrastructure of the country is down, propane and kerosene will not be delivered, but wood is all around us.

4

Food Storage 101

Where to start? That is more a question to me as I am writing this more so than one for you. I had the extreme privilege of growing up in a household where both parents lived through the Great Depression. Both my mother and father were raised on a farm in Kentucky during the Depression. One thing we never were short of in our house was food. My mother, God bless her, still buys in large quantities even with just her and Dad to prepare for. But, growing up poor in the Depression, I believe it was a learned behavior in them to store as much food as they could. They never went without food on the farm. This was due not to government handout programs but hard work and preparation. The summer was a time of growing and storing as much food as possible to survive the winter. Food storage has been instilled into me from a young age. Growing up we always had a full pantry, we always grew a garden, we always canned, and we always stored food. Looking back at the summer afternoons shelling beans didn't make sense to me at the time but now I look back and thank God for giving me the parents I have and the lessons they taught me. I hope that some day my children will reflect back in the same manner. One of the funniest things my Dad ever said to me when I asked him how the Depression had affected him, he said, "Son, we were so poor, we didn't know anything was different." That seems to be some of the problem that we are facing in today's modern world. Where the majority of the families of the Depression went to the store once a month, we can't make it 2 days. This chapter will help you to develop an attitude of food storage. It is a train of thought in as much as anything else. It never ceases to amaze me how far we as Americans have removed ourselves from the standards that were so prevalent during the Depression. The majority of the households in the United States probably have less than a week's worth of food stored. I am not just speaking of people at below poverty level; I am talking about people who are currently making in excess of $100,000 per year. There is no excuse for anyone not to have at least a three-month supply of food.

During the great scare of Y2K, thousands of people went out and bought a years supply of food in 5 gallon buckets. Some paid an astronomical price for this storage food not even knowing what they had or how they were going to use it. Most of these supplies have either been sold at a garage sale, thrown away, or sitting in the corner of a storage room gathering dust. One of the goals of writing this book is to better educate you on what foods to store, how to store them, and how to use them. The main idea that we have to remember is store what you eat and eat what you store. That sounds simple, but so many people trying to get ready for Y2K bought hundreds of pounds of rice, beans and wheat. Now there is not a problem with buying those things if you know how to use them and like them. There is no sense in buying 500 pounds of pinto beans if you don't like them. Or they bought a thousand pounds of wheat and didn't own a grinder, or didn't like wheat bread. It reminds me of a quote from Robin Williams, *"The first time I tried organic wheat bread, I thought I was chewing on roofing material."* Some of my bread has come out exactly like that. That is why I made it a purpose in life to find good recipes and use them to make sure we number one, liked it, number two we can make it. Just like standing in a garage doesn't make me a Cadillac, neither does buying a cookbook make me a cook.

Let's Get Started

First things first, you need to assess your current food storage. Basically, what do you have on hand right now? Do you think you have enough food for your family to last a week without going to the store? How about a month? What we are going to try to work towards, as a basic start, or the first building block, is three-month supply of food. That may sound like a lot, but how much life and health insurance do the experts recommend? FEMA (Federal

Emergency Management Agency) only suggests 3 days of food in their *Are You Ready? An In-depth Guide to Citizen Preparedness* (IS-22). As we all have seen in the past, 3 days worth of food will not be sufficient during some of the larger catastrophes. Speaking to someone who recently went through Hurricane Ike in Houston, 3 days is definitely not enough. It was weeks before some people had power restored. It was over a week before the stores were up and operational in some areas. That is just one instance, one difference is that if the continental United States comes under attack, or civil unrest escalates, there will be no re-supply trucks rolling in.

Now that we have looked at our current situation, and seen that it is lacking, what is the next step? Just like going to a restaurant, Menu please. Most never know what they are going to eat for dinner tonight much less next week. This is where the planning and paperwork begins. Sit down with either a computer or a piece of paper and pen and write down a menu for one week for your family. If you are accustomed to eating out, don't be disheartened. It is actually easier for someone who is not use to cooking than someone who cooks quite a bit. Both my wife and I cook a majority of our meals from scratch. We use fresh ground cornmeal and flour. But, a lot of times we don't remember exactly how much of each ingredient we put into our meals. Starting off from scratch is not what we are going to be going after. Our main goal is keep our cost down and have some palatable food. The target price is $2.00 maximum per person per meal. With two dollars, you can buy two hamburgers, or two tacos off the dollar menu at some of the fast food restaurants. Not with our menus. And if you say you don't have the time, how long does it take you to drive to that fast food restaurant, order the food, wait for them to serve you, and then drive home. Not only is it more time consuming, what about the cost of the fuel and the use of the vehicle. Many of the recipes we list here are as fast or faster, better for you, and cheaper.

By keeping our cost low, we can effective save more money to store more food. If we keep our cost below $2.00 per person lets look at the math.

4 people x 3 meals a day x $2.00 = $24.00/per day

$24.00/per day x 7 days = $168.00 per week

$168.00 per week x 12 weeks = $2016.00

Now for $2000 you can have 3 months worth of food for your family. Remember that the $2.00 is the maximum on the meals. Some of our meals are around $1.25 or $1.50 per person. At $1.50 the cost is reduced by $504 to make it $1512. Again, this doesn't have to be purchased all at the same time; it can be bought over time.

There are some really good software programs out on the market today. We use Cookbook Wizard. It can import most other software recipes, and there is a multitude of them on the web. I believe we have over 3000 different recipes on it. Some of the features include looking up by ingredients or name, and making a shopping list. This is where it comes in handy for planning your menu. Be forewarned that some of the recipes that are brought in off the internet will not format correctly for your shopping list. If you put your recipes in though there shouldn't be a problem.

Planning a weekly menu is a win-win situation. How many times have you stood and looked in the refrigerator and wonder what you are going to cook. Or have you ever got a craving to cook something and find that you are missing some of the main ingredients? With the menu planned out, you know what you are going to cook ahead of time. And, if your better half doesn't like what is on the menu, let him plan it. In all honesty, sit down together and plan it out. When my wife and I first did this, we looked at each other in amazement at how few meals we really had in our repertoire. Since then we have added quite a few. Start basic. If your family likes chili, you can have chili with hotdogs, chili pie, chili Mac, etc. With one base you can have four or five different meals. I don't think it would be advisable to have them all in the same week though. Look at soups and mixes at the first. They are more expensive than making them by scratch, but just like anything in life, take small steps. We can start with both canned and fresh meat, and then we can progress to totally canned meat. This is not to say that we have to limit ourselves to only canned meat, because it is more expensive than fresh usually. Also, when I am speaking of canned meat, I am not just speaking of Spam™ and Vienna sausages. There are some very good canned meats on the market with some long shelf life that are ideal for the pantry. List the meals on the chart for each meal each day. Once you have the menu established, then list out the ingredients for each meal. I know that this is time consuming, but it is well worth it.

Let's take a look at chili for the first. We can make a meal of canned chili and cornbread. This is a filling meal and fairly inexpensive. We are going to start with the easiest combination, no scratch work.

Chili with Cornbread

Chili		
2 can	Chili with Beans	$2.00
1 can	Chili Hot Beans	$0.60
Cornbread		
2 pkgs.	Jiffy Corn Muffin Mix	$1.25
2	eggs	$0.35
1 can	cream style corn	$0.60
1/4 cup	vegetable oil	$0.10
3/4 cup	shredded cheddar cheese	$0.50
	TOTAL	**$5.40**

Mix the cans of Chili and Hot Beans in a saucepot and cook over medium heat for approximately 15 minutes or until hot.

Preheat oven at 350°. Spray a 10" skillet with a non-stick spray or use bacon grease and coat the skillet. Mix the dry cornbread mix, eggs, corn, oil, and cheese in mixing bowl until it is the consistency of pancake batter. Pour batter in skillet and bake for approximately 20 minutes at 350° or until a toothpick comes out clean.

As you can see, there is a recipe that will feed four for $1.35 per serving. Now how does this figure into our food storage? The next time you go to the grocery store, buy four cans of chili for $4.00, and then buy two cans of chili hot beans for $1.20, two cans of cream corn for $1.20, and finally four packages of Jiffy corn meal mix for $2.50. These are the staples that you can store in the pantry. You have just spent $8.90 before tax for the majority of two meals.

Tuna Salad

3 cans	Tuna with water	$2.10
1lb pkg.	Macaroni Noodles	$1.50
1 jar	Sweet Relish	$1.50
1 jar	Mayonnaise	$2.50
6	Eggs	$0.75

Boil the eggs, cube. Prepare noodles as package directs. Drain water from tuna. Mix ¾ cups of mayonnaise, 2 Tbs. of sweet relish, drained tuna in bowl. Drain noodles and rinse in cold water. Mix eggs, noodles, and tuna together in bowl. This is great served with chips or crackers.

I listed the full cost of the sweet relish and mayonnaise in the cost, but you will only use a portion of it. The rest can be stored in the refrigerator for later use.

Now on your next trip to the market, buy nine cans of tuna for $6.30 and 3 lbs. of Macaroni Noodles for $4.50. You now have the staples for 3 meals at $10.80 before taxes. This is also not taking into consideration of bulk purchases or sales, which we take advantage of every chance we get. For $19.70 you now have a total of 5 meals for 4 people. This is what I call the $20 per week plan. Basically you can take an extra $20 per week and budget it into buying your pantry staples. If $20 is too much, then break it down to $10 a week. If you do this for a three-month period or 12 weeks, you have spent a total of $240 and have the ingredients for 60 meals. Remember I am using just these two meals as examples. But with 60 meals at your fingertips that can be used for both lunch and dinner you now have a month of lunches and dinners for a family of four. The items listed above will store for a minimum of one year. When you are buying pantry items, try and find the longest shelf life on the items. Most are printed on the can or package. Grocery stores usually rotate the older items to the front. I can't count the number of times that my wife has had me reach to the very back of the shelf to retrieve the newest stock, but it is worth the extra effort.

We have already discussed the tuna and the chili, which are a good start, but now let's move to other items. Soups are always a good buy. There is a multitude of them on the market. As with anything that you haven't tried, buy one first and see if you like it. The condensed soups are the best bargain. Here is a list of basic soups with recipes.

Cream of Mushroom

- Tuna Noodle Casserole
- Creamy Chicken with Noodles
- Creamy Ham with Noodles
- Creamy Tuna on Toast
- Rice Casserole with Ham or Chicken

Cream of Chicken

- Chicken Noodle Casserole
- Chicken Pot Pie
- Chicken and Rice
- Baked Chicken with Almonds
- Plantation Ham Pie

Cream of Celery

- Ham Casserole
- Ham and Biscuit Casserole
- Ham and Potato Slow Cook
- Slow Cook Chicken

We usually use the house brand soups for cooking with and the name brand for eating by themselves. Experiment on your own. With the soup and some canned tuna, chicken or ham, and either noodles or rice, you can have a few meals. Listed below are 7 different recipes that use common items and can be made from canned and dry items. At the end of the recipes will be a shopping list to make all seven and total cost.

Recipes for Storage

Ham Casserole

1 lb	can ham, diced
1 cans	condensed cream of celery soup
½ cup	milk
1 can	potatoes, sliced
¼ cup	onion, dehydrated
2 Tbs	grated Parmesan cheese

Preheat oven to 375 degrees. In an 8x8 inch casserole dish, combine cream of celery soup with milk. Layer potato slices, onions and ham on top and cover. Bake for 1 hour. Remove cover and sprinkle with parmesan or other grated cheese. Bake uncovered for another 20 minutes.

The soup will cost $1.00, the milk can be condensed and will cost $1.50, potatoes $.70, and the ham will run $2.50 and the Parmesan cheese approximately $.50. Total cost will be $6.20. An added addition would be a half-pound of rice that can be steamed or boiled separate and the casserole served over. The rice would increase the cost to $6.85 for 4. The cost is still well below the $2.00 mark at $1.71 each.

Here is another variation of the Ham Casserole.

Creamy Ham Casserole

1 lb	ham, can cubed
2 cans	potatoes, sliced
1 cans	condensed cream of celery soup
½ cup	onion, dehydrated
2 Tbs	butter
2 Tbs	flour, all-purpose
1 tsp	mustard, ground
½ tsp	salt
½ tsp	pepper
1 ½ cups	water
1 cup	Cheddar cheese, shredded

Place the potatoes first, then the ham, then sprinkle the onions on top in a slow cooker. Melt the butter in the saucepan then stir in the flour slowly, then the mustard, salt and pepper to make the rue. After the rue is smooth, combine the soup and water in a bowl, and then slowly stir into the rue. Bring the rue to a slow boil; simmer for a few minutes until it has thickened. Once the rue has thickened, pour over the ham and potatoes in the slow cooker. Cover and cook for 4 hours. Sprinkle the shredded cheese over the top before serving.

The ham is $2.50, the potatoes are $1.20, the onions $0.80, the butter is $0.25, the cream of celery soup is $1.00, and the cheddar cheese is $1.00. The other ingredients costs are negligible but for argument sake lets set them at $0.50 total. Total cost is $7.25.

Ham and Biscuit Casserole

1 lb	ham, can cubed
½ cup	onion, dehydrated
2 Tbs	butter
1 can	condensed cream of chicken soup,
1 can	condensed cream of broccoli soup
½ cup	dehydrated milk
¾ cup	water
1 can	carrots, sliced

Topping

2 cups	biscuit/baking mix
½ cup	water
½ cup	parsley flakes
Min.	flour for rolling dough

Preheat the oven to 425°. Spray a 13" x 9" baking dish with non-stick spray or coat with oil. Place the ham and carrots in the bottom of the dish. Re-hydrate the dehydrated milk. Melt butter. In a separate bowl combine soup, milk, butter, onions, and pour over ham. Combine biscuit mix and water until dough forms. Knead dough until it is not sticky on a floured surface then roll out into a 12" square. Sprinkle the dough with the parsley then roll into a jellyroll. Cut the roll into 10 or 12 pieces and place on the mixture in the dish. Place the dish in the oven and bake, uncovered for approximately 30 minutes or until the biscuits are golden.

The ham will cost $2.50, the onion $0.80, the butter $0.25, the cream of chicken and broccoli soup $1.40, the carrots $0.50, and the baking mix $0.40. Total cost $5.85.

Slow Cook Chicken

1 can	chunk chicken breast
1 can	condensed cream of chicken soup
1 can	condensed cream of celery soup
1 can	condensed cream of mushroom soup
½ pound	white rice

Drain chicken in cans. Add chicken, cream of chicken, celery, and mushroom soup, and the rice in a slow cooker. Cook on for 2-3 hours on medium. Note: the soups are the 10.75 oz cans.

The chicken cost is $2.00 per can, the soups are approximately $1.00 per can, and the rice is going for $1.00 per pound. Total cost of the meal is $5.50 for four. It is still below our range of $2.00 per person.

Baked Chicken with Almonds

2 can	chunk chicken breast
1 can	condensed cream of broccoli, undiluted
1 can	condensed cream of chicken soup, undiluted
1 cup	mayonnaise
2 cups	Cheddar cheese, shredded
1 tube	crackers, Ritz style (approx. 20 crackers)
1/4 cup	butter, melted
1/2 cup	almonds, sliced

Spray a 13" X 9" baking dish; place the chunk chicken in the bottom. Combine both soups and mayonnaise in a bowl then pour over chicken. Crush the crackers then combine with the butter. Sprinkle the cheese and then the crackers on the top. Place the almonds on the top then place in a preheated oven at 350°. Bake for 1 hour or until golden brown.

This recipe makes 6 servings. Chicken is $4.00, soups are $2.00, the mayonnaise approx. $.75, cheese $1.75, crackers $.35, butter

$.50, and the almonds $1.25. Total cost $10.60 or $1.77 each. A lower cost can be achieved by dropping off the almonds. The price shown here for the almonds are the small bags, try to buy these in bulk, you will realize a dramatic savings.

Chicken Pot Pie

1 can	Chunk chicken, 13oz
1 can	condensed cream of mushroom soup
1 can	condensed cream of chicken soup
¼ cup	onion, dehydrated
½ can	chicken broth 7oz.
1 can	potatoes, sliced
1 can	carrots, sliced
¼ cup	butter
¼ cup	flour, all-purpose
4 oz	evaporated milk (1/2 cup)

Preheat oven to 400° F. Drain the chicken, then combine the chicken, cream of mushroom and chicken soup, the onions, broth, potatoes, and carrots. Stir together. You can season to taste with salt and pepper. Pour into 1-quart baking dishes. Begin making the rue by melting the butter in a small saucepan and then stirring in the flour. Once the rue is mixed well, stir the milk in and whisk until all the lumps are removed. Pour the mixture over the chicken in the baking dishes. Bake for about 1 hour. Serves 4.

The chicken is $2.00, the soups are $2.00, the onion is approximately $0.40, the broth, potatoes, carrots are $1.80, the evaporated milk is $0.80, the butter is $0.50, and the flour is roughly about 3 cents. Total cost is $7.53. We use canned evaporated milk, carrots, potatoes, and onions en lieu of fresh, but you can substitute fresh if available.

Creamy Chicken and Rice

1 can	Chunk chicken, 13 oz.
1 can	Condensed cream of chicken soup
1 can	Condensed cream of celery soup
2 cups	Rice (approximately 1 pound)
1 can	Condensed Milk
1 cup	Water

Either steam or boil the rice. Then combine the chicken, cream of chicken, and cream of celery soup, condensed milk and water in a pot on medium heat. Cook for approximately 20 minutes or until just starting to boil, stirring to keep it from sticking. Once boiling, mix rice in and stir. Simmer for 5 minutes. Serve in bowls. Makes 4 servings.

The chicken is $2.00, the soup is $2.00, the rice is $1.30, and the condensed milk is $0.80. Total cost is $6.10.

Tuna Noodle Casserole

1 lb	egg noodles
¼ cup	butter
1 can	condensed cream of mushroom soup
1	can tuna, drained (5oz.)
¼ cup	milk
1 cup	Cheddar cheese, shredded

Boil a large pot of water, add pasta and cook until al dente. Bring a large pot of lightly salted water to a boil. Cook pasta in boiling water until al dente, and then drain. Melt the butter in the same pot then add soup, milk, tuna, and cheese. Stir mixture until the cheese has melted. Add pasta to mix, stirring in until evenly coated.

All of the recipes that are listed above are for a family of four. Remember, this is not going to be a stuff yourself until you can't walk properly buffet style meal. We have become a nation of excess in all aspects. I am always amused when on the rare occasion we eat fast food and someone in line orders the large size of hamburger, the largest french-fries, and then a diet Coke™.

As with any of the meals listed here, add side items that are filling but inexpensive. For instance, two packages of flavored Ramen noodles can be made and served as a soup at the first. Total cost around $0.25 total. Then as a side dish that is extra filling try and boil rice or noodles. Two cups of dry rice will equal approximately four cups of cooked rice. That is enough for 1 cup of cooked rice per person. Two cups of rice is close to one pound or another $1.00 at high retail prices. The last bulk rice I bought was $21.00 for 50 pounds. That makes the cost only $0.42 per pound.

SHOPPING LIST FOR 10 MEALS (FOR 4)

MEAS		INGREDIENT	TTL	
1	Pkg	Almonds, sliced	$	1.25
1	Box	Biscuit/baking mix	$	2.00
1	Lb	Butter	$	2.00
1	Can	Carrots, sliced	$	0.60
2	Lb	Cheddar cheese, shredded	$	4.00
1	Can	Chicken broth 7oz.	$	0.50
4	Can	Chunk chicken breast 13oz.	$	8.00
2	Can	Condensed cream of broccoli soup	$	2.00
4	Can	Condensed cream of celery soup	$	4.00
5	Can	Condensed cream of chicken soup	$	5.00
3	Can	Condensed cream of mushroom soup	$	3.00
3	Can	Condensed milk	$	2.40
1	Box	Crackers, Ritz style (approx. 20 crackers)	$	1.50
5	Lb	Flour, all-purpose	$	2.00
1	Box	Grated Parmesan cheese	$	2.50
3	Can	Ham, can cubed lb.	$	7.50
2	Jar	Mayonnaise	$	5.00
1	Box	Mustard, ground	$	1.00
1	Lb	Onion, dehydrated	$	4.50
1	Can	Parsley flakes	$	1.00
1	Can	Pepper	$	1.00
4	Can	Potatoes, sliced	$	2.40
2	Lb	Rice (approximately 1 pound)	$	2.60
4	Can	Tuna with water	$	2.10
1	Lb	Macaroni	$	1.50
1	Jar	Sweet Relish	$	1.50
2	Can	Chili with Beans	$	2.00
1	Can	Chili Hot Beans	$	0.60
2	Box	Jiffy corn mix	$	1.50
1	Can	Corn, cream style	$	0.60
1	Lb	Egg noodles	$	1.50

TOTAL $ **77.05**

Now the prices above are current at the writing of this book, in the spring of 2009. They also do not take into account the discounts you can achieve in buying on sale and in bulk. Now you have a list to get started with. If you buy $20 per week of the items listed above, in four weeks you have stored ten meals for four people. Continue doing this every week but using your own recipes and in six months you should have 60 meals for four people.

By following these examples above you can have your food storage program up and running.

BASIC MENU LIST

	Breakfast	Lunch	Dinner
Monday			
Tuesday			
Wednesday			
Thursday			
Friday			
Saturday			
Sunday			

5

Hardcore Food Storage

What is hardcore food storage you may ask yourself? This is where we store up more than just the basic 3-month supply of food for emergencies. This is the food stores that will allow your family to survive major catastrophes. It will take dedication and perseverance to achieve, but once it is, the peace of mind is priceless. If you have the money to buy your family's one-year food supply, well, God bless you. But, it is going to be hard for a company to know what your families likes and dislikes are. But if you are starting like we did, frugally, then this is your chapter, so lets get started.

Below is a list that is similar to the LDS (Latter Day Saints) one-year storage calculator except we have modified it to better fit our family's usage. The food calculator is a good starting point but it just didn't cover everything needed. Now the amounts on this list are for one person and are only a reference. We will take each category and discuss it in detail. Some of the items may work for your plan, some may not. Again, use my list and adapt it to your own family.

Food Storage for One Year for One Adult

Grains			Fats and Oils		
Wheat	100 lbs.		Shortening	4 lbs.	*olive oil*
Corn	25 lbs.		Vegetable Oil	2 1/2 gal.	
Oats	23 lbs.		Shortening, Powder	44 oz.	
Rice	45 lbs.		Peanut Butter	4 lbs.	
			Peanut Butter Powder	13 oz.	

Sugars			**Cooking Essentials**		
Honey	4 lbs.		Baking Powder	1 lb	
Sugar	40 lbs.		Baking Soda	2 lbs.	
			Yeast	1 lbs.	
Legumes *(wash)*			Salt, kosher or pickling	5 lbs.	
Beans, dry	60 lbs.		Salt, table	5 lbs. *sea salt*	
			Vinegar, White	4 gals.	
Misc.			Vinegar, Cider	2 gals.	
Pasta, Dry	15 lbs.				
Fruit, freeze dried	1 lbs.		**Milk**		
			Dry milk	50 lbs.	

Grains

Before storing grains, there is one piece of equipment that must be purchased, that is a grinder.

Grinders

There are not many uses for the grains we store without the grinder. Just like purchasing a new vehicle, buying a grinder has many choices. There are manual grinders and electric grinders. There are grinders that are manual that can be converted to electric. There are big ones and small ones, plastic models and steel models; the list goes on and on. Their price range covers just about as wide of spectrum, from $60 to over $500 each.

The parts of the grinders are basically the same. They consist of a hopper which is where the grains are poured in and fed to the grinding apparatus. Next is the grinding apparatus which is one of three types, steel burrs, stones, or impact. Then there is the mechanism to rotate the grinding apparatus which is either a handle for manual or a motor for electric.

After reading many reviews on the different electric grinders, we chose the Nutrimill Grain Mill which is an impact grinder. We based this decision on numerous customer reviews on the internet. After working with the mill I have not had any problems. It doesn't grind as fast as manufacturer claims but it does grind very fine. We have used it for corn, wheat, and beans without any problem. It has been reviewed as the quietest electric mill on the market, but to me it sounds like a jet engine while running. We use the Nutrimill exclusively to grind our wheat and corn. Usually I will try and grind a weeks worth of grain at one time. What I don't use to bake with immediately, I pour into Ziploc bags and store in the freezer. Remember that the whole grain will not go bad but the flour will go rancid rather quickly.

The Nutrimill is a little pricey at $270. But, the quality of flour that you can grind is almost untouched on the market today. I recently saw a five pound bag of whole wheat flour going for over $6.00 and cornmeal for over $5.00 for a five pound bag. I believe that once you try your own wheat and meal you will not want anything commercial again. The flavor just can't be beat. As we have discussed in the previous chapters, always have a backup. This holds true, especially when considering a grinder. If you just purchase an electric model, what happens when you have no more power? That is why we chose the Family Grain Mill as a manual grinder. This decision was again made after reading many customer reviews on the internet. For the price, the Family Grain Mill is hard to beat. It costs $120 but stands up to the higher price models. Straight out of the box this was a little dynamo. It went through corn with hardly any effort. One great advantage to the Family Grain Mill over the impact grinders like the Nutrimill is that oily seeds such as sesame or peanuts do not cause any problems. The major downfall is that it will not grind fine enough for bread flour with one pass. It takes me approximately 30 minutes to grind 5 cups of wheat with the Family Grain Mill. That time includes

running it through twice. We looked at the other manual grinders but due to either their cost or quality chose the Family Grain Mill. One manual grinder worth mentioning is the Country Living Mill. Many swear by it as the best manual grinder. It can also be converted to run with an electric motor. After looking at the Country Living Mill I believe that it will outlast me and my children. The only holdback with the Country

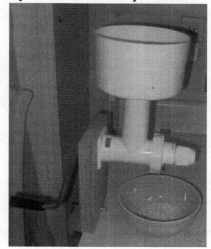

Living Mill is its price at $400, and that is without the electric conversion.

Like purchasing a car, everyone has their own preferences. Just don't bank your whole bulk grain grinding on a $20 grinder.

Wheat

It is no mistake that wheat is listed at the very top of the list. Wheat is a staple that your food storage plan should not be without. There are two types of wheat, red and white. Of these there are different varieties, hard and soft and spring and winter. This can get really confusing. So here is a chart and the common uses of each.

TYPE	USAGE
Hard Red Winter	Bread, meat extender
Hard White Winter	Light Bread
Soft White Spring	Pastry, cereal
Soft White Winter	Pastry, cereal

The most popular wheat found on the market is hard red winter. The hard wheat stores better than the soft wheat. Also, the soft is not recommended for making yeast bread. The red is a fuller wheat flavor when making bread. We mix our white and red when making bread for our own mix. As you become accustomed to making bread you can experiment as we did to find the best flavor combination. The list calls out for 150 pounds per person for a full year. That may seem like a lot but let's take a look at how it will be used. One of our favorite recipe for bread calls for 12 cups of flour to make four loaves. That is 3 cups of flour per loaf. A family of four will consume approximately 1-½ loaves of bread per day on an average. That is 4 ½ cups of flour per day. One pound of wheat berries equals approximately 4 ½ cups of flour when ground. One pound per day equals 365 pounds per year for four people. That only equals 91 pounds of wheat per person. The calculations used here are only for making bread, there are other uses for wheat than bread. One such use is boiled wheat berries. This can be eaten for breakfast similar to oats with some honey, milk and a little cinnamon. Or, it can be used as a substitute for potatoes or rice in a dinner. So, **100 pounds of wheat is an appropriate amount per person per year** as a minimum. We can store 36 pounds of wheat in a 5-gallon bucket. That means that you need to have 3 buckets per person on average. Store in 5-gallon buckets with mylar bags, oxygen absorbers, and a well fitting lid. Always freeze the grains for at least 72 hours to kill any bugs or larvae in them. We also add a bay leaf and diatomaceous earth to aid in the prevention of insects. I will show how to store foods in the buckets at the end of this chapter.

One word of caution, start slow when using whole-wheat products. We have become so use to the refined dust that the stores sell for flour that an actual large amount of whole wheat in some diets can wreak havoc.

Flour

Contrary to the list, I don't believe in storing flour. Flour has a limited shelf life compared to whole-wheat berries. Once the wheat has been ground, if not refrigerated or frozen, within 72 hours, 90% of the nutrients will be gone due to oxidation. While on the other hand the wheat berries can be stored almost indefinitely.

The flour that is available in the supermarkets is so far removed from the actual wheat berry it should be a crime. Most of the nutrients and vitamins are removed from the wheat berry with the wheat germ. Have you ever seen wheat germ for sale in a health food store? That's why; the healthy part of the wheat is removed and sold to make people healthy. Up until the 1920's the white flour sold was not enriched. But by 1942 the United States Army restricted the purchasing of un-enriched flour. Some interesting facts about white flour are that cockroaches or ants will not eat it. For an experiment, when you find a line of ants on the sidewalk outside, take some white flour and spread a line across them. They will walk all the way around it to avoid it. Then take some whole wheat that you have ground and do the same thing. They will flock to it as fast as their little legs will take them to it. This tends to tell me that if God gave the insects the wisdom to know better than why don't we have the same sense.

Cornmeal/Corn

I regard the storing of cornmeal in the same category as storing flour. Cornmeal like flour will store longer in the seed form as God intended. The product that you can buy in the supermarket is similar to wheat flour, the outer skin and germ has been removed along with most of the nutrients. Home ground cornmeal seems to have more flavor to it also. The cost is also a great savings when you grind your own. A fifty pound bag contains approximately the same amount as 8-½ 5-pound bags of cornmeal that if you bought at the supermarket at an average price of $2.50 each. The bag of corn cost approximately $7, a savings of $14.

We store shelled dry corn. This is the same product that is fed to livestock. Contrary to what some may say, it is safe for human consumption. It can be found at your local feed stores. Just check to see if it has been cleaned and also checked for aflatoxins.

The majority of the feed corn is called "dent" corn. This is from the dents on the side of the seed after it has dried. The other type seen is called flint corn. Flint corn is a close relative of popcorn. It is very hard and some grinders will not handle it. I have never used popcorn but have heard from others that it is grittier than the dent corn.

Cornmeal has many uses in your food storage. Cornbread can be added to many meals to stretch the food. It is nutritional and filling. Corn tortillas, corn muffins, and fried flat breads.

If we make just 3 pans of cornbread per week, with our favorite recipe, that would require 6 cups of cornmeal. Four cups of whole corn weighs approximately 1-½ pounds and after ground contains approximately 5 cups of cornmeal. That means that we need to have 2 pounds of corn per week or 100 pounds per year for four people. The 25 pounds of corn per person is adequate for your storage needs.

Oats

Most Americans consider oats as only a bland breakfast meal. Many of us have not to fond memories of being made to eat it when we were kids. But, oats have many other uses than breakfast. Oats can be added to meat to extend it. Oats can also be ground into flour with your grinder and used in breads and pastries. And, we can't forget oatmeal cookies, my favorite. Oats are also very high in nutritional value and are quite filling. Most supermarkets carry quick oats and old-fashioned oats. The only real difference is the thickness of the oats. Old fashioned or thick rolled oats seem to have more flavor than the quick and the instant. If oatmeal were eaten everyday, it would require 2 cups of oats per day. Two cups of oats weigh approximately .4 pounds. That equals 146 pounds of oats for four people for a year, or 36 pounds per person. I think that total is a little high, for one thing, I don't believe I could stomach oatmeal every morning. A standard 5-gallon bucket with mylar bag can hold approximately 23 pounds of oats. That is a good number per person.

Rice

The versatility, high calorie content, long shelf life, and still relatively inexpensive cost makes rice one of the top staples for you to store. There are so many uses for rice that entire books have been written on just such. Our family uses rice for all three meals. A good hearty breakfast can be made with rice in the form of rice pudding. Fried rice is a family favorite in our house. We use white rice as a side serving to extend the meat frequently. Many of our casseroles call for rice also as an extender. I have also noticed that some of the Mexican fast food restaurants are using rice in their bean and meat mixtures. Like I stated earlier, the versatility is untouched by any other food item.

There are two types of rice, brown and white. White is what is commonly stored. White comes in three different varieties, Long grain, medium grain, and short grain. Long grain is the most common. Long grain is at least as three times as long as it is wide. Medium grain is at least two times as long as it is wide. It seems to be stickier when cooked. Short-grained rice is less than two times as long as it is wide and is sometimes called "sticky rice" due to the way it cooks. We store the long grain in larger quantities than the short grain.

Storage of rice is identical to the other grains that we store. Rice doubles when cooked, so one pound of rice equals two pounds cooked. Most recipes for fried rice call for one cup of uncooked rice for four people. One cup of rice weighs about half a pound. If we cooked a serving of rice each day that would be equivalent to approximately 180 pounds of rice for four people or 45 pounds per person per year. We can store 36.5 pounds of rice in a 5-gallon bucket.

Sugars

Honey

Honey has been used for food since the beginning of time. We see that in Exodus the Israelites were well familiar with honey.

And the house of Israel called the name thereof Manna: and it was like coriander seed, white; and the taste of it was like wafers made with honey.
Exodus 16:31 (KJV)
Also, we see that when Christ arose from the grave and appeared before the apostles He also ate honey.

And they gave him a piece of a broiled fish, and of an honeycomb.
Luke 24:42 (KJV)

Honey occurs 56 times in the King James Version of the Bible. Needless to say, it was an important staple during those times. Now it has been relegated to use on biscuits in America. Very few use honey in common foods. Just as the wheat berries are in my opinion better for us health wise, so is the honey. Honey has been well documented as a natural energy booster, an immunity builder, and a remedy for a wide range of ailments from yeast infections to arthritis.

Now that I have proclaimed the benefits of honey, what can we use it for in food storage you may ask?

We have been using it for our bread for quite sometime now. Most baking recipes can have honey substituted for sugar. Some cooks add a pinch of baking soda to offset the acidity of the honey and help prevent scorching.

How much do we need to store? Our recipe for bread requires a ¼ cup of honey for 4 loaves of bread. If we consume 1-½ loaves of bread a day, this works out to approximately 8 ounces of honey per week. That computes to 16 pounds of honey per year or 4 pounds per person as a minimum. Due to the longevity of storage, I would suggest at least 6 pounds per person. For reference, honey is sold by the pound, not the gallon. A cup of honey is approximately 12 ounces. A gallon of honey weighs 12 pounds. Always buy raw local honey. The raw honey is free of any additives that the larger companies may add. Also, it is claimed that the local honey helps with your immune system.

Refined Sugar

Our modern day table sugar has been so refined that except for moisture and vermin it is pretty much indestructible. The minimum required amount per person of 40 pounds per year is an acceptable amount. When purchasing, be sure and check the pricing of both the large and small bags. The small can sometimes be found on sale for 20 cents per pound. Once you have purchased it, storage will be the next concern. A 5-gallon bucket will hold 45 pounds of sugar. Always store with mylar bags, oxygen absorbers and a good sealing lid on the bucket. If the slightest moisture gets in, you will have a 5-gallon brick of sugar.

The other sugars like brown or confectioners sugar store in the same manner as the refined sugar. The need for them in your food storage again is a personal preference. Our main stores for sweeteners are honey, refined white sugar, and brown sugar.

Legumes

Legumes or dry beans are another item that should not be overlooked. Beans are very versatile, store well, are quite healthy and are relatively inexpensive.

The different types of beans are just as numerous as their uses can be. They can be used in soups, as a side dish, as a meat substitute, and even ground into flour and used in bread. The majority of beans that we store are pintos, navy, great northern, black, and chickpeas. These are the varieties that my family likes.

But others store black-eyed peas, lima, and kidney just to name a few.

One of the great advantages beans have is being on both the meat and bean section and the vegetable section of the food pyramid. A ¼ cup of cooked beans is equivalent to 1 ounce of meat with an average of 15 grams of protein per cup; beans make a great alternative to meat. According to a study by the USDA released on June 23, 2004, beans rank at the top of the list for antioxidants. Antioxidants are disease-fighting compounds. Beans are high in fiber and good source of protein. They are also cholesterol, fat and sodium free. Below is a list of common beans and their nutritional value.

Based on 1-cup of cooked beans.

Bean Variety	Calories	Protein	Fat	Carbs	Fiber	Calcium	Iron	Potassium
Fava	187g	12.9g	0.68g	33g	9.2g	61mg	2.6mg	456mg
Navy	258g	15.8g	0.1g	16g	10g	128mg	4.5mg	670mg
Pinto	235g	15.8g	0.1g	44g	7g	81mg	4.5mg	495mg
Black	227g	15.2g	0.93g	41g	15g	46mg	3.6mg	611mg
Great Northern	209g	14.7g	0.8g	37g	12.4g	120mg	3.8mg	692mg
Garbanzo	269g	14.5g	4.3g	45g	12.5g	80mg	4.7mg	477mg

Storage of beans is identical to the storage of grains. Dry beans are readily available in the large supermarkets all over America. Variety may be limited though in the supermarkets. Some other good places to find different varieties are at ethnic stores. The Mexican stores will have different types of pintos and black beans while the oriental stores may carry different types of soy and mung. Again, what you store should be what you are accustomed to eating.

One pound of beans equals approximately 2 cups dry and when cooked equals 4 to 5 cups. When making white bean soup for my family, I usually use one pound. If you serve three meals a week with beans, that would be 156 pounds of beans for four people for a year or approximately 40 pounds per person. Forty pounds would be the minimum but I still suggest having at least 60 pounds per person. A typical 5-gallon bucket will hold roughly 35 pounds.

Shop around for the best deals and you can save a considerable amount.

Pasta

This is another staple that most do not include in long-term storage but we do. We use pasta in extending the meal. It is relatively cheap, and will store well under the right conditions. Most can be purchased for under a dollar a pound. One pound of dried pasta cooked equals about one and half pounds of fresh pasta. Pasta does not have as big of yield as rice or beans have, but it will add variety to your menu.

Pasta needs to be stored in a cool, dry place. It is recommended that it be removed from its original packaging and repackaged in either a Ziploc or vacuum-sealed bag with oxygen absorbers. Then the bags need to be placed into a 5-gallon bucket. The 5-gallon bucket is a good deterrent from rodents, insects, and water. If stored in the process described previously, the pasta should last from 8 to 10 years. I would suggest a minimum of 60 pounds of dried pasta for a family of four or 15 pounds per person for a year.

Fruits

Fruit is also another staple that should be added to all preparers' lists. Most canned fruits will store from two to three years with no problem. Bargain stores like Dollar Tree, and Family Dollar Store usually have a very good selection of fruits from strawberries to peaches for a dollar a can. I suggest trying to store at least one serving a week of fruit for each person. This can be accomplished both with canned and with freeze-dried varieties. There are so many varieties of freeze dried fruits now that it is amazing. At one time, you could only find bananas and apples. Now there are strawberries, raspberries, peaches, and blue berries. These all make a great addition for baking and just eating by themselves. It you regulate yourself to a cup a week say in a muffin mix, you would need 3 #10 cans.

Fats and Oils

There are many trains of thought concerning fats and oils in our diets. Regardless whether the experts agree or disagree that we need to have fats in our diets, remember we are talking about long-term storage and hard times. I don't believe that if we are using our long-term food storage we will be worried about trans-fats. Some of the ways we need to look to our storage needs is by taking clues from our forefathers who didn't have a Wal-Mart around the corner. Most of the lists that I have read about concerning the provisions that the pioneers took on the Oregon Trail always had at least 50 pounds of lard on them. It was generally used for cooking, in biscuits, and occasionally used for wheel grease. Although we probably will not have a need for it on our wagon wheels, we will need some type of oil and fat in our storage. Most bread recipes call for butter, oil, shortening, or some type of fat. Oils will be needed to fry with also. We average 10-gallons of cooking oil a year for four people. The main problem with trying to store fats and oils though is their short shelf life. It has been suggested to only store vegetable oils for one year although, we have personally used some that was considerably older. Trust me; you will know when it has turned bad as soon as you open the lid. Canned shortening has about a two-year shelf life, but it also can be extended over that. Another good choice is to store cooking spray. They also like the shortening have at least a two-year shelf life. A great alternative for long-term storage is shortening powder. Shortening powder is basically dehydrated soybean oil. It has a shelf life of about 15 years. It can be mixed into bread dry or rehydrated en lieu of oil. It also can be sprinkled on the skillet and as it warms up it melts and coats the skillet for frying. We store all three in our provisions. Remember as we have spoken all through this book, have a primary, a secondary, a third and possibly even a fourth or fifth. Always have a backup. I suggest storing at least 2 ½ gallons of cooking oil per person, four pounds of shortening per person, and two 44 ounce (#10 can) of powdered shortening per person.

Mayonnaise and Salad Dressing

I am the first to tell you that I am country. One of my favorite sandwiches, just like David Letterman, is a bologna sandwich. We joke and call bologna "Tennessee Round Steak." And no self respecting country boy would eat a "boloney" sandwich without mayonnaise. With that being said, the shelf life of mayonnaise is usually about one year unopened. But a good alternative is making your own. We have made our own with the eggs from our chickens but have also experimented with using freeze-dried eggs.

Homemade Mayonnaise

2 Tbs	Whole Egg powder
4 Tbs	Water
1 ½ Cups	Vegetable Oil
1 Tbs	White Vinegar
1 tsp	Prepared Mustard
pinch	Salt

Reconstitute the eggs by blending them with the water in a mixing bowl with a whisk. If doing this by hand, add a drop of oil to the eggs and whisk vigorously. Continue adding one drop of oil at a time until the mixture begins to thicken. After adding approximately a ¼ cup of oil, add the vinegar and beat into the mixture. After the vinegar has been mixed in, the remainder of the oil can be added in a steady stream, all the while whisking. Once all the oil has been beaten in, add the mustard. If the mixture is too thick, a few tablespoons of boiling water can be whisked in to thin. Chill the mixture, and store in the refrigerator for the maximum of 4 days.

Peanut Butter

Peanut butter is a good source for calories from fats, carbohydrates, and protein. This lends itself to an energy food. Most will store for up to two years without any problem. Try and store at least four pounds per person of canned peanut butter.

Another good source for peanut butter is peanut butter powder. This is dehydrated peanut butter that you have to add water to reconstitute it. When reconstituted it will be a paste perfect for spreading on bread or using in a recipe. It will store for approximately 5 years unopened. There is nothing like a peanut butter and homemade jelly on homemade bread sandwich.

Cook Essentials

Cooking essentials are basically the ingredients needed to make some of the recipes. This can be a very extensive list in itself.

Leavening Agents

Leavening agents are added to bake goods before baking to produce carbon monoxide that causes the baked good to 'rise.'

Baking Powder

Baking powder is a leavening agent mainly used in baking, hence the name. Baking powder is a combination of baking soda, an acid salt such as Cream of Tartar, and a drying agent such as cornstarch. The mix will determine whether it is "Single" or "Double" action. Single action begins to react in the bowl; double reacts in the bowl but also reacts in the dough when it begins to cook.

Most recipes call for a small amount for baking but make those recipes for over a year and it will require a substantial amount to store. Most can be stored for a year and a half unopened. Although we have used some that was over three years old and it still worked. If in doubt, take a small amount and put in a bowl and then pour hot water in the bowl. If good bubbles start to form, it is still good.

Baking powder can be found in one-pound cans. Store at least one pound per adult for a year as a bare minimum. Single action baking powder can be made with ½ teaspoon cream of tartar, 1/3-teaspoon Baking soda and 1/8-teaspoon salt = 1 teaspoon Baking powder.

Baking Soda

Baking powder is pure Sodium Bicarbonate. Baking soda reacts to acids by effervescing (fizzing); this creates the carbon dioxide to help the product rise. Baking soda also has a myriad of other uses. It can be used to put out a grease fire by throwing handfuls on the flame. One of the most common uses is for a freshener; we have all put them into our refrigerator to reduce smells. It can also be used as a sunburn relief when made into a paste with water. It is suggested to store at least one pound per adult per year, I personally try to keep at least 2 pounds per person due to its versatility. One good thing about baking soda is that if it is stored properly, in an airtight container at room temperature, it will store indefinitely.

Yeast

This is by far the most popular leavening agent. This is what makes your bread rise. We use approximately ½ ounce for four loaves of bread. If we eat 1 ½ loaves a day as we discussed earlier, then we need approximately 1 ¼ ounces per week or 4 ¼ pounds of yeast a year for four people. A good amount is one pound per adult a year.

Salt

Salt

Salt has been a vital ingredient in life since the beginning of time. Salt has made and destroyed many empires. It is more than just that little shaker on your table. Salt contributed to civilization with its preservation qualities allowing people to travel with stored food. It still has the same preservation qualities today, we just don't use them. It has been shown in studies that too much sodium in our diets is bad for us. But, again we are talking about bad times coming, and we will need salt in preserving different foods. We store two types of salt, table salt and canning salt. The canning salt is just a coarser grain salt and is used in brining and curing meat, and in pickling. If kept in a moisture free container, it will store indefinitely. I suggest storing a minimum of 5 pounds of pickling or kosher coarse grain salt for a year and a minimum of 5 pounds of salt per person of table salt. Store in a mylar and bucket combination. It still is currently only about $.33 per pound so there is no excuse not to store enough.

Vinegar

We mainly use vinegar during the summer for pickling. Distilled white vinegar and apple cider vinegar has many other uses besides pickling. Vinegar is used for everything from killing weeds to soothing a sore throat. Most of our pickling recipes call for at least a cup per quart in pickling. As you begin to store your own food, pickling will come into play. Opening a quart jar of bread and butter pickles or jalapeno relish in December is a treat within itself.

If you use a cup per quart and plan on putting up 40 or 50 quarts then you are going to need at least store 3 to 4 gallons of distilled white vinegar and at least 2 gallons of apple cider vinegar for a family of four. One good thing about vinegar is that it will store almost indefinitely.

Spices and Flavorings

This is also another overlooked item that should be listed as a necessity. The proper use of spices can make the basic foods dare I say tolerable and even likable. Steamed rice is at its best filling and all right without spices, but adding a chicken or beef spice mix to it makes it palatable. So without a doubt store as many spices as you can. A great place that we have purchased bulk spices from in the past is Atlantic Spice Co. that is located Massachusetts.

The best way to store the spices are to separate into ¼ pound increments and then use a vacuum sealer to protect them from any air from getting in. Then store the ¼ pound bags in a mylar bag and 5-gallon bucket with lid. This should keep it protected from vermin and water. Some guides have suggested that spices lose their effectiveness after one year. We are still using spices that we have stored over 10 years ago and they still are very potent. I would love to offer a tablespoon of my 10-year-old cayenne pepper to the experts to eat and see if they would change their opinion.

The different varieties of spices we store:

- Allspice
- Basil
- Black peppercorns
- Bouillon, Chicken
- Bouillon, Beef
- Cayenne pepper
- Chili powder
- Cinnamon powder
- Cinnamon sticks
- Cloves
- Cumin
- Dill
- Garlic powder
- Mustard powder
- Nutmeg
- Onion powder
- Onion flakes
- Oregano
- Paprika
- Parsley
- Rosemary
- Sage
- Thyme
- Vanilla bean

Notice that we do not store mixes like taco seasoning or bbq seasoning. We mix these ourselves with the ingredients listed above.

Chicken Rice Mix

1 Cup	rice, uncooked
1 Tbs	instant chicken bouillon
¼ ts	salt
1/8 ts	onion, minced
½ ts	thyme
1 Tbs	parsley
1/8 ts	pepper
¾ ts	sugar

Boil 3 cups of water; add 1 cup of rice mixture, cover and simmer for twenty minutes or until the liquid is absorbed. Makes two cups.

Chili Seasoning

1 Tbs.	Paprika
2-½ Tbs.	Salt
1 tsp.	Onion powder
1 tsp.	Garlic powder
1 tsp.	Cayenne pepper
1 tsp.	Black pepper
½ tsp.	Thyme
½ tsp.	Oregano

Mix ingredients together, store in an airtight container. Use 1 tablespoon per pound of hamburger used in chili.

Taco Mix

1 Tbs.	Flour
1 tsp.	Chili powder
1 tsp.	Paprika
3/4 tsp.	Salt
3/4 tsp.	Onion minced
1/2 tsp.	Cumin
1/4 tsp.	Cayenne pepper
1/4 tsp.	Garlic powder
1/4 tsp.	Sugar
1/8 tsp.	Black pepper

Mix ingredients together, store in an airtight container. Use 2 tablespoons per pound of hamburger.

These are just some of the mixes that can be made from your stockpile of spices to add more variety to your stored foods.

Dairy Products

Not many people think about dairy products in their long-range storage plans. But, milk is needed for making bread and other recipes. Unless you have access to dairy cows or goats, it is going to be hard to have fresh milk and milk products. This is where freeze-dried products come in handy. Dried milk is not a new product. Marco Polo wrote of the Mongolian Tartar troops carrying sun-dried skimmed milk in their stores.[4]

---

[4] p 262 in "The Book of Ser Marco Polo, Book 1" translated by Sir Henry Yule (3rd edition), Charles Scrabner's Sons, New York, 1903

We use dried milk in the making of our family bread. One cup of dried milk weighs approximately 2 ½ ounces. If we use 2/3 cups of dried milk for four loaves of bread, and we consume 1-½ loaves a day, we will have to store approximately 30 pounds of dried milk for a family of four just for the bread. This does not even take into account any for drinking. If each member of the family drinks just one glass of milk a day (approximately 2 cups), then the amount needed would increase tremendously by 150 pounds. I believe that a minimum of 50 pounds per person should be stored.

There are three types of dried milk:

- Nonfat, which is dried pasteurized skim milk
- Whole, has a higher fat content, but shorter shelf life
- Buttermilk, used mainly in baking, and even shorter shelf life

The instant nonfat dried milk is relatively easy to find, most supermarkets have it on the shelves. The majority of it usually comes in a cardboard box. This is not a good way to store it. Dried milk is highly susceptible to moisture and odors. There are many companies that sell it in #10 cans on the internet. I wouldn't suggest purchasing it in the five or six gallon pails unless you have a large family that will use it rather quickly. The average shelf life of nonfat dried milk is approximately two years if unopened and stored in 70° or less. After opening, place in an airtight container and refrigeration will extend the shelf life of the dried milk.

Another fine substitute that we have used extensively is Mountain Mills Milk Substitute, which is a whey based milk substitute that can be used in the same way that the nonfat dried milk is used. It actually has a better taste than some of the nonfat dried milks that we have tried.

Speaking of taste, I would suggest trying different brands before buying your supply. We did numerous taste tests before we settled on the Mountain Mills substitute.

Another item that should be purchased along with the dried milk is a mixing pitcher. This pitcher has a plunger that aids in the mixing

of the milk and also increases the oxygen, which helps to improve the flavor. Also, try and mix the milk the night before to aid in the flavor. The flavor is not as good as fresh milk, but again we may not be in a position to have fresh milk.

How to Store Bulk Grains

Here is a pictorial guide of how we store our grains.

Step 1

First step is to place the mylar bag into the bucket.

Step 2

Next pour the grain into the mylar bag.

Step 3

Place the oxygen absorbers and bay leaf in the mylar bag with the

grain. We are storing corn in these pictures so we use two of the 500cc oxygen absorbers. One about half full, the other at the top. Conversion is at the end of this chapter.

Step 4

Now we seal the bag. We use a hair straightener we picked up for

a few dollars at a garage sale. They make sealers specifically for this purpose, but the straightener does the job. Some use a clothes iron, towel and board.

Step 5

Now that the bag has been sealed, place the lid on the bucket and use a rubber mallet or the palm of your hand and seal the bucket. Last thing to do is label the bucket of the contents and the date.

If you have followed these steps, your grains should be safe for about 15 to 30 years. Remember, that temperature is a very big factor in the storage of your food. The average temperature should be 70° F.

Shelf Life at 70° F

Item	Years
Black Eyed Pea	15
Corn	10
Great Northern Bean	20
Lentils	20
Mung Bean	10
Navy Bean	20
Oats, Rolled	30
Pinto Bean	20
Rice, white Long Grain	10
Salt	Indefinitely
Spaghetti	15
Sugar	Indefinitely

The times are again based on keeping the buckets at 70°. For approximately every 10° F that the temperature changes, it will greatly reduce or increase the shelf life by a factor of two. Simply put, if a bucket of corn is kept at 80° then the 10 years expected at 70° has now become 5 years. 10 divided by 2 equals 5. But, if the bucket were kept at 60° then the corn's shelf life would jump to 20 years. To illustrate how the heat will destroy your food though, that same corn kept at 90° the shelf life will only be 2.5 years.

What Can Fit in a 5-Gallon Bucket?

ITEM	POUNDS
Black Eyed Pea	31.5
Corn	37.5
Great Northern Bean	35
Lentils	35.5
Mung Bean	37.5
Navy Bean	37.5
Oats, Rolled	20.5
Pinto Bean	24
Rice, white Long Grain	36.5

These weights are approximate of what we have been able to store in a 5-gallon bucket with a mylar bag.

To figure how many CCs of oxygen absorbers you will need for a 5-gallon bucket, some math will be needed. We will use corn for an example.

There are 453.6 grams per pound. Convert the pounds that you are putting into the bucket by multiplying the pounds times 453.6. From the list above,

37.5 lbs. x 453.6 = 17010 grams

This gives you the amount of grams in the bucket.

To determine our headspace and void space in the bucket,

There is 18,942 cc of volume in a 5-gallon bucket. We subtract the grams of the corn from the volume of the 5-gallon bucket.

18942 cc - 17010 g = 1932 cc residual air volume

There is approximately 20.5% oxygen in air. So to remove the oxygen, we have to multiply the residual air volume by 20.5%.

1932 cc x .205 = 395.06 cc oxygen volume

This shows that we need at least a 400 cc oxygen absorber.

If you don't want to work the formula above, a good rule of thumb for 5-gallon buckets is 3 each 500 cc oxygen absorbers per bucket when storing items that have more density and less air such as grains, flours, wheat, flour, and rice. For items like pasta and beans which have less density and more air, use twice the amount or 6 each 500cc oxygen absorbers. This is a little bit of an overkill, but rather safe than sorry.

6

The Little Things in Life

The little things in life are what make life more enjoyable. We have discussed the major items needed to survive a major event, but the little things that we have and use during a day are what make survival turn into living. Here is where we need to think of the items in life that we use everyday that aren't associated with food, water, and shelter. One early lesson I learned about the little things of life and not having them was the first time that I went on maneuvers with the U.S. Army. The old adage, "You don't miss the water till the well runs dry," holds true. This lesson should be learned and adapted to your family before a major event.

I will try and cover some of the items that we keep on hand, but each family will be different. Use the examples that are given here and expand on them to incorporate into your family's lifestyle.

Personal Hygiene

The old saying, "Cleanliness is next to Godliness" cannot be found anywhere in the Bible but it does have its merits. The first time that it was used in English was in the writings of Francis Bacon albeit slightly different. In his 'Advancement of Learning' (1605) he wrote: "Cleanness of body was ever deemed to proceed from a due reverence to God."

What? know ye not that your body is the temple of the Holy Ghost which is in you, which ye have of God, and ye are not your own?

1 Corinthians 6:19 (KJV)

We see that Paul told us that our body is the temple of God, who wants a dirty church? I am sure that I am preaching to the choir, but this is one area that many people do not consider when thinking of survival. Personal hygiene has some basic ingredients in the recipe. A hot shower can go a long way in improving morale. If you don't believe me, start taking cold showers. It is not unheard of to take cold showers. One of the best showers I ever had was in the swamps of Georgia at Fort Stewart where I took a five gallon water can and poured it over my head. We can take cold showers in a survival setting, but if we can have a hot shower with a bit of forethought, why take a cold one. In the last few years, the camping equipment suppliers have come up with a great invention. It is a portable shower. There are a couple of different types and they cost anywhere from $10 to $250. The $10 variety is a 5-gallon black bag that is hung up in the sun to heat the water and it uses gravity for the flow. The problem with this one is it only works in warm weather. The other types are actually battery-powered pump with a propane heater for the water. Coleman has come out with the Hot Water on Demand system. It is a small self-contained unit that will heat and pump the water. It is relatively expensive averaging $250 and still requires the additional purchase of a spray adapter to us as a shower. It will heat 40 gallons of water on one 1lb. canister of propane, and the pump's battery is rechargeable. It is a good solid unit, but again rather expensive. Another brand is the Zodi Hot Tap. This unit sells for around $125 and requires no other additional items except for the water, batteries, and fuel to have a shower. It will

heat up to 60 gallons of water on one 1lb. canister of propane. The Zodi is the best value for the dollar. It also has an optional bulk fuel connection kit available so that the unit can be operated with a 5-gallon propane tank. Remember how we discussed

utilization of identical fuels, this lends to the propane fuel as your primary. The unit can also serve double duty to heat water for washing utensils, coffee, and soup. It would be a good addition to your equipment.

Toiletries

Now that we have discussed the hot water for the shower we need to consider the soap and shampoo. This is another item that many people do not store an adequate supply of. An average bar of soap should last one person 3 weeks. Now the math is relatively simple. If one bar last 3 weeks then it will take approximately 17 bars per person per year. For a family of four we are talking about 70 bars of soap. You can buy a bar of soap for $.50 or less on sale, that would be $35 out of pocket expense to have a year supply stored. Shampoo usage is very hard to predict for each family due to how much hair you have. Now for some of us men that are getting up in age, one bottle of shampoo could last all year. But in all honesty, monitor how long it takes to use a bottle and multiply it by the number of weeks.

Deodorant is also another item to look at. If a container of deodorant lasts you two months, then store at least 6 bars per adult. Trust me everyone will be grateful for this stock.

Toothpaste and toothbrushes also need to be stored. There are always coupons in the paper to help purchase these items at a significant discount. Try and store at least 4 toothbrushes per person for a year.

Some other items to be considered are feminine hygiene products. Try to store a year's supply.

Toilet Paper

This is a serious item that needs to be stored. Just like the shampoo and toothpaste, each household's usage can and will be different. We average two rolls of toilet paper per day with a family of six. This does not take into consideration that some toilet paper may be used by members of the house while they are away from home. So we concluded that 3 rolls per day would supply us. We have been able to store a 6-month supply but anymore than that will take a new storage site. A large supply of toilet paper will take a considerable amount of room. For a family of four that uses 2 rolls per day a year's supply is equivalent to 182 4-roll packs. One way that we have cut down on the size factor is to actually crush the rolls. Just smash the rolls down so the inner tube will become flat. It makes it harder to roll out, but most will not complain due to having some toilet paper at a crucial moment.

Entertainment

This is another item that many people over look. Depending on how long the event lasts people can get cabin fever. There are different types of entertainment today. I believe our society is 90% entertainment and 10% work. The entertainment I am mainly speaking of requires no electricity. This will be strange to the last couple of generations, but people did entertain themselves before television, DVD, X-Box, and PSPs. I remember when growing up that there would be card-playing parties at our house from time to time. The adults would play Rook or Spades or Hearts for hours on end. We kids were relegated to Go Fish or Poker if our mommas didn't catch us. Cards are a very cheap form of entertainment. Buy a couple of decks of regular playing cards and some of the unique card games like Rook, Uno, or Phase 10. Just for fun, schedule a card night and play games with the kids instead of sitting in front of the television. We have become so alienated from our own family members with our lifestyles now; you might just have fun with each other if you try it. Another cheap entertainment is board games. There are a multitude of them on the market that are really inexpensive. Dominoes should also be considered especially if you have younger children. My mother taught my children to play dominoes by the age of five or six. Dominoes provided entertainment for them even younger by using them for building blocks. Books also fall into the category of entertainment. Try and pick up a series of books in a genre that you like and put back for just such an occasion. The problem I keep running into is that I read the books as soon as I acquire them. But, I save them in the hopes that someone else in the family might like to read them. There are many electronic games on the market that use AA batteries. These can also be purchased and use rechargeable batteries but I tend to swing towards the use of non-electronic entertainment due to having another set of batteries to charge.

Laptop Computer

Many are seeing this topic and wondering how it fits in to survival. With the leaps and bounds we have made in technology in the last ten years, a laptop can provide many different things for a family.

The first and foremost use will be for information. This information could be anything from books on disk to your important papers. Right now is the best time to start committing your personal papers and pictures to disc. If something happens to the hard copies of your papers without a backup it will be up to you to secure copies. What are some of the papers you need to commit?

1. Birth and Death Certificates
2. Marriage License.
3. Social Security Cards.
4. Titles to property owned.
5. Insurance policies, these should include automobile, house, life, and health.
6. Wills.
7. Immunization Records.
8. Diplomas, training records, awards.
9. Resume.
10. Tax records.
11. Special Licenses.
12. Receipts for major purchases.
13. Dental records.
14. Optometrist records.

All of these items need to be scanned and saved to the hard drive first and then to either a DVD or a memory stick. A word of caution, with all of your vital information on one disk, if it fell in the wrong hands it could be devastating. Take some precautions and encrypt the information. There is a very good encryption program on the market called TrueCrypt. It is a very good encryption program that will give you peace of mind and one of the best features about it is the cost, it is free. Their website is located at http://www.truecrypt.org/.

Once your main documents have been recorded, the next items should be your photographs. There are probably many photos that have been taken of your family over the years that just couldn't be replaced. Now is the time to start recording these memories to disk. Using a computer and a scanner, start copying the photos. It will take a great deal of time, but it is well worth it if the originals are destroyed. Once you have recorded all the information on the media, place that media whether it is disks or memory sticks in a safe place. In a safe is the best location. Also, put a copy in a place that is offsite. This could be a safe-deposit box at the bank or in a friend's safe. Don't worry about security if you have encrypted your files.

Another use for the laptop is for entertainment. The newer models have a DVD player where you could watch movies or play games and be entertained. With a small inverter the laptop can be charged thru the automobile cigarette lighter. They can be purchased for under $500 presently.

7

All that Glitters is not Gold

As we have been discussing in the other chapters, it is imperative that we tackle getting prepared in small steps so as not to be overwhelmed by it all. The stockpiling of silver and gold is a step for the advanced preparer. For as many experts that there are in preparedness, there are as many opinions about precious metals. Some stress stockpiling as much as you can, others state that you shouldn't have any. I am right in the middle. Not trying to avoid the argument, I feel that there is a place for PMs (precious metals) in everyone's plans. To expound my feelings further, I am a firm believer in securing other items first before any PMs are purchased. The market will wait. Even if you see the price of silver drop to $5.00 per ounce, if you don't have any food stored, then the silver is not, and I repeat NOT a good buy. Don't look at it as a good investment for later down the road, you can't eat it. I didn't see one instance of silver and gold being used for tender in New Orleans after Katrina. The stockpiling of PMs is for long-term survival. The PMs that we have acquired are viewed as a hedge when all Federal notes have been exhausted, and we have nothing else to barter with. Think of them as a last ditch effort. That is why I don't look at them as a "have to have" item in my preparations. Again, I am not against the ownership of PMs, just in the proper time frame. Now let's discuss the different ones that are out there.

Silver

We will start with the cheapest of the PMs. Silver comes in an array of articles to collect. The first we will discuss is junk silver. Junk silver is a term for any coin, which contains silver in it, but due to its condition it has very little numismatic value. In other words, it is not rare or in very good condition. Its value lies in the silver that it contains solely. The most commonly collected U.S. junk silver coins are the Roosevelt dimes, Washington quarters and Kennedy halves. All of which have a date of 1964 or before, except for the Kennedy halves, which we will discuss later. All of the dimes, quarters, and halves that were minted in 1964 and before contain 90% silver. That means that the coin was minted with 90% silver and 10% clad, or other metal. When new, the coins contained .7234 ounces of silver per dollar of face value. Due to circulation, the silver content is reduced due to wear. That is why it is assumed that there is .715 ounces of silver per dollar of face value. Now the Kennedy halves took a different road in minting than the other coins. From 1965 to 1970 the Kennedy halves were minted with 40% silver content. Therefore they hold less value due to the lower percentage but they still hold a place in the junk silver category. There is approximately .148 troy ounces of silver in one Kennedy half from 1965 to 1970. Using the table below, you can determine the value for the face value of silver coins. Just add the quantity of the items you have in the Qty column, put the current spot price in the Spot column, then multiply the Qty., by the Factor, then by the Spot to get what your silver is worth.

TYPE		QTY	FACTOR	SPOT	TTL
1916-1945 Mercury Dimes			0.0723		
1946-1964 Roosevelt Dimes			0.0723		
1932-1964 Washington Quarter			0.1808		
1916-1947 Walking Liberty Half			0.3617		
1948-1963 Franklin Half			0.3617		
1964 Kennedy Half			0.3617		
1965-1970 Kennedy Half			0.1479		
1878-1921 Morgan Dollar			0.7735		
1921-1935 Peace Dollar			0.7735		

The percentage of silver per coin is shown without the wear factor being figured in. The going prices should be approximately +/- 10% of the calculation.

So if you had a roll of assorted 1932-1964 Washington quarters then you would calculate as such:

40 Quarters x .1808 x spot (as of writing this $10.82) = $78.25 uncirculated.

40 Quarters x .1788 x spot $10.82 = $77.39 junk price.

With markup $78.25 x 1.10 = $86.08

So, if spot is at $10.82 and you can find a roll of quarters between $75 and $85 it would be an average price. If you can but them like I have from the bank for $10.00 each, face value, then by all means buy all that you can. The bank still gets silver coins in all the time. It helps to become friendly with your tellers. In the past I have bought customer rolled coins from the bank to sort through looking for silver. Odds now have steadily decreased in finding silver due to others doing the same thing, but every so often I do run up on them. Most of the silver I have acquired I have purchased well below the current spot price. The best place to check on the spot price of silver is www.kitco.com. They not only have the pricing on silver but also gold and platinum.

When it comes time to sell, there are a few avenues to take. Sell or barter to a private individual will net you the largest gain and is my favorite avenue. Then I would list Craigslist as number two due to you are still dealing with private individuals without any charges for selling. Number three would be Ebay. Ebay has such a large audience so your odds are greater in selling but you will have to set up an account with both Ebay and Paypal, and will have to pay to list and sell your items, and also be charged to accept payment from Paypal. The next and last avenue to consider is to sell to a dealer. One thing you should remember especially when selling to dealers is a lesson an older man taught me many years ago, it doesn't matter what some book says something is worth; the real value of an item is what someone will actually pay you for it. So don't be disheartened if you go to sell some of your silver coins and the dealer offers you 25% below spot what it is worth. This is not anything derogatory against dealers; remember they are in business to make money.

I believe that the most bang for the buck will be junk silver. The reasons for this opinion is that it is easily recognizable, hard to counterfeit, and in the different denominations it makes it easier to use than a solid ounce of silver. A good example is that you could trade a dime and quarter, or 35 cents face value easier than cutting off a piece of a silver bar or ingot and weighing it. We will discuss the bars and ingots later and why I don't really like them.

Silver Eagles

There is one fairly new silver coin that the United States has minted that I haven't covered yet, and that is the silver eagle. The U.S. Mint began in 1986 minting a one-dollar coin called the silver eagle. Even though it has one dollar stamped on it, it is worth a considerable amount more than one dollar. It was originally minted for the numismatic society but the preparedness movement began to store them also. The silver eagle is a beautiful coin in itself, and each one contains at least one troy ounce of .999 silver. The only down fall of the silver eagle is that it trades dramatically over spot value. At the current spot rate of $10.82, the eagles are trading on E-bay at $17.00 to $18.00 each. This makes them a very non-frugal purchase for preparedness. Again, if you have your preps in order and want to purchase some then by all means buy some. But my suggestion is to swing towards the junk silver due to some of the same problems we discussed earlier about a large piece of silver.

Silver Rounds, Ingots and Bars

When I first starting investing in silver, I bought the generic silver rounds at first due to the price difference. Rounds are usually cheaper than U.S. mint coins over spot, so that makes them attractive to the frugal preparer. But, after much thought, I will not buy any silver bullion other than that minted by the United States. The reason being is that the problem with the rounds, ingots and bars is that they are not familiar to the general public. Only a small percentage of the populous trade in PMs currently, these would be the only ones that could tell an Engelhard Silver Prospector from a shiny piece of alloy. Without being a trained assayer and having assaying equipment it would be hard for me or anyone else to distinguish between silver and another alloy.

Gold Eagles
The United States Mint authorized the American Gold Eagle in 1985 as an official gold bullion coin. The first coins were minted in

1986. They are in denominations of $5, $10, $25, and $50. The corresponding weights are 1/10 oz., ¼ oz., ½ oz., and 1 oz. respectfully. All four contain 91.67% gold (22 karat), 3% silver, and 5.33% copper.[5] Again like the Silver Eagle, they are a beautiful coin, but they command a premium over spot, which in turn represents a non-frugal purchase. To reiterate, these come at the end of the journey of preparedness not the beginning. They do have a place though in your stockpile for long-term investment to be used in a long-term survival situation. You can purchase the Gold Eagles at the same places that the other PMs can be obtained. Remember, like everything, and especially when you are buying in bulk, shopping around can save you some major money.

Final Notes on PMs
I guess I am still old school though, silver and gold feels like something tangible, not like the Federal notes that we get at the bank.

But the PM market is very volatile. Not as volatile as the stock market. Ask people who own Ford and GM stock. If in 1920 you received a $20 gold piece, you could have bought a nice tailored suit. Today that same $20 gold piece would buy you a very nice tailored suit. If you would have received a $20 federal note, you couldn't buy the pants let alone the suit. Gold is about as close of an object as can be found to be inflation proof. It is volatile market

---

[5] http://www.goldline.com/coins/product/american-gold-eagle.html

as a previously said; I remember buying silver at $4 spot and then in a few years seeing it jump to $20. I usually get an itch to start buying more when I see the price climbing. If you get that urge, fight it with all your being. As history has shown, it will come down again, and we haven't run out of it yet. I will repeat, ONLY purchase PMs when you have your other preps in order. That is hard advice to follow, even for the author. But, don't do it. Buy it after you are comfortable with your food supply, your water source, your energy source, your land, your.... I could keep going, but I think you get the point.

8

In Defense of a Nation or Just your Family

I mentally wrestled with this subject for quite a while not knowing whether to put it in this book or not. Many take a different view about defense and Christianity than I. So, if you do not believe in self-defense and protecting your family, I'll only ask you to keep an open mind as you read this. I again feel it is my duty to first warn my brothers and sisters, and secondly inform them to the best of my ability. We purchase thousands of dollars of insurance each year but trust that the police will be there when someone wishes to do us harm. Who knows, maybe your opinion could change, I pray that it does. Remember what my brother Peter told us.

Be self-controlled and alert. Your enemy the devil prowls around like a roaring lion looking for someone to devour.

1 Peter 5:8 (NIV)

Our enemy the Devil also has many soldiers out there ready, willing and able to do his bidding. I won't even quote any of the recent newscasts that show all the death and mayhem happening in our country right now. If you watch the evening news at night you have already seen them. Not taking anything from our police force, they do a good job, but there is just too much area and too many crimes for them to be there all the time. According to the Department of Justice survey of Crimes in 2006, you have a 25% chance that it will take over an hour for the police to arrive on the scene.[6]

So how does a Preacher of the Gospel maintain a conviction that we are to defend ourselves? Many will ask if I have forgotten Jesus telling us to turn the other cheek in Matthew 5. Jesus meant that if someone deeply insulted us, than don't pay it back with another insult. I don't believe that Jesus meant if someone physically attacked you and yours than do not protect yourself. Jesus himself did not turn his cheek in front of the Sanhedrin.

When Jesus said this, one of the officials nearby struck him in the face. "Is this the way you answer the high priest?" he demanded. "If I said something wrong," Jesus replied, "testify as to what is wrong. But if I spoke the truth, why did you strike me?"

John 18:22-23 (NIV)

---

[6] Criminal Victimization in the United States - Statistical Tables Index, http://www.ojp.usdoj.gov/bjs/abstract/cvus/response_time_to_victim584.htm

Jesus didn't turn His cheek but asked why was He assaulted. In Luke, Christ warns His disciples that they would be facing hostility in the future.

He said to them, "But now if you have a purse, take it, and also a bag; and if you don't have a sword, sell your cloak and buy one. 37 It is written: 'And he was numbered with the transgressors'; and I tell you that this must be fulfilled in me. Yes, what is written about me is reaching its fulfillment."

Luke 22:36-37(NIV)

Notice that He didn't tell them that they needed to turn the other cheek; he asked if they had a sword. If they didn't, then sell a coat and buy one. I don't know of any other way to interpret this but that Jesus advocated self-defense. Now some of my counterparts will bring up the incident in the garden where Peter, trying to defend Jesus, utilized his sword and cut the ear off of the high priest's servant, Malchus. Jesus told Peter to put his sword back not because what Peter had done, but that Jesus knew His time had come.

I am not advocating that we begin our own crusades and exterminate all the infidels. What I am advocating is that there may come a time in the not too distant future that we may have to defend ourselves from enemies both foreign and domestic. I like to make the playing field as level as possible for myself and my other brothers and sisters in Christ. The only way I can do it for them is provide as much information as I can and hope and pray you weigh the consequences if you do not arm yourself. In the Gospel of John, Jesus spoke of some of today's current problems.

They shall put you out of the synagogues: yea, the time cometh, that whosoever killeth you will think that he doeth God service.

John 16:2 (KJV)

Disclaimer

Before any weapon is acquired and fired, I highly recommend that at a minimum a firearm safety course be taken. There are plenty of good ones out there. I guess the Harvard of firearm courses would be Frontsite. More can be found on their website at http://www.frontsight.com. Also, you can check with the NRA on their website for classes that are in your area. A good place to start is at

http://www.nrahq.org/education/training/basictraining.asp.

The other part of this disclaimer is directed towards the weapons that are discussed. These are my personal preferences. This is in no way a total encompassing volume of all the different variations of weapons that are on the market today. Some of my choices may not be your personal choice that is why they make so many different kinds. To use an old cliché, "to each his own." If you like Berettas instead of Glock, or AK47s instead of AR15s, then by all means stick to what you know.

Where to Start?

If you have ever gone into a major gun store and looked at all the choices of weapons that are out there, you could be overwhelmed. I have been shooting since I was big enough to hold a weapon. I have shot everything from black powder to fully automatic weapons. I have used a firearm in the protection of my life more than once. I thank God that I have never had to take a life. What I will try to do in this next chapter is explain what choices will benefit you and why.

First Weapon

My first choice for anyone that doesn't currently own a firearm would be a 12ga. shotgun. The reasons for choosing a shotgun are relatively simple:

- They are fairly inexpensive.
- They are readily available.
- Their ammunition is also readily available.
- The public does not perceive them as an evil weapon.
- They do not require a lot of practice to be proficient.
- With the proper loads, they will not penetrate sheetrock walls.
- They are a multi-tool capable of self-defense and acquiring game.
- They deliver maximum damage at close range.

There are basically four types of shotguns. They are single shot, double barrel, pump and automatic. The single shot is probably the cheapest out there. They can be found for as little as $50 for a break barrel single shot. They are very reliable for the cost; the only downfall is that you have only one shot. I have killed plenty of small game in my younger years with a single shot 12ga.

The double barrel is basically the same as the single shot except with two barrels. There are two configurations of double barrels. There is an over and under which has one barrel stacked on top of the other. Then there is the side by side, which has two barrels next to each other horizontally. Double barrels are also very reliable and increase your capacity to two shots. Many bird hunters use double barrels like the Ruger Red Label with great proficiency. The double barrel also has a significant psychological factor if you are staring down the business end of it.

The next model of shotgun is the pump action. This is my personal

favorite. I guess I was fifteen when my father bought me a Remington 870™ Wingmaster. I probably could fill the bed of my pickup truck with the squirrels, rabbits, and dove I have killed with it. I have never had a malfunction from any of my pump shotguns. They are very reliable and have the added benefit of a magazine tube. A standard pump shotgun will normally hold five rounds with the plug removed. Most states have a law against having over three rounds in a shotgun while hunting, but that is not applicable to keeping one in the house for protection. I suggest taking out the plug while using it for home protection with a small side note. Put the plug in a safe place where you will remember it when you go hunting or you might be like me one time when I got to the dove field and then remembered the plug. I scrounged a pencil out of the console of my truck and cut it down so that it would work. Good thing I did because the game wardens came by that morning and checked our weapons. There are many different brands of pump shotguns on the market today. I personally like the Remington 870 Express™ or the Mossberg 500™. They have been sold at many of the discount stores such as K-Mart and Wal-Mart and the availability of the parts is more than satisfactory. Many can be found at the pawnshop for as little as $125 each. I have bought several between the $100 and $150 price range. All were well used with some battle scars but still functional and very dependable.

The last model of shotgun is the automatic. I have owned a few automatics in the past. They have been somewhat reliable. When I say this, I mean that some tend to be finicky about the rounds you use. One such was an SKB automatic that would jam up. But in the same aspect, I had a Remington 1100™ that shot anything I threw at it. Automatics are also like the pumps in that their standard capacity is usually five rounds.

Now that we have discussed the different types of shotguns, let's discuss the gauges. They're the .410, the 20ga, the 16ga, the 12ga., and the massive 10ga. In years past there were also 8ga. and 6ga. The .410 is a small shotgun round thus producing a small shot pattern. The 20ga. is immensely larger than the .410

and very popular. The advantage of the 20ga. over the 12ga. is that the recoil is significantly less. Many smaller framed people like the 20ga. due to this fact. With the lower recoil, confidence in hitting the target can be achieved due to not being afraid of the kick. The most popular gauge is the 12ga. The 12ga. is my favorite round. The shells can be found at just about any discount store and are usually the cheapest. The 12ga., just like the others, can be used with game loads for hunting and buckshot for self-defense. The 12ga. does have a significant kick with some magnum shells. One thing that I have noticed though is that when I am shooting dove, I don't seem to notice the kick as much as when I am shooting skeet. I firmly believe that if you do have to use a shotgun for defense, you won't notice the recoil. The only reference I have to the 10ga is that of duck hunting. Many of my friends use the Remington SP-10™ so that they can have a large shot pattern. I cannot agree with the added cost of the weapon and the rounds for the difference in the shot pattern for self-defense.

Now that we have discussed the models and the gauges, I hope that I have not thoroughly confused you. There are many other factors that I haven't even discussed. We haven't looked at the different chokes, the different manufacturers or the barrel lengths. Like I said at the beginning, there are a lot of different choices.

My Recommendations

For home defense, I have the same shotguns for every grown member of the family. That is the Remington 870 Express™ in 12ga. It is a no frills, matte finished workhorse. On the different shotguns we have numerous barrels. My favorite for bird hunting is a 26" with screw in choke tubes. Due to it being shorter than the 28" or 30" standard I am able to acquire the targets faster. For home defense, we use the 18" barrel with the magazine tube extension. This allows for easier movement in close quarters with the shorter barrel, and allows for the addition of two more shells. This gives a capacity of 7 rounds. That is a considerable amount of firepower. We don't use the pistol grip stock configuration due to the punishing kick of the 12ga. rounds on the hand. Trust me you will feel it in the web of your hand if you shoot many with a pistol grip. If you can find a Remington 870 Express™ fairly cheap but it has the 28" barrel, go ahead and purchase it. Additional barrels can be bought later. Next, I would purchase different types of shells. I would start with a minimum 250 rounds of #6 or #7 ½ game rounds in 2 ¾" shells. These are the most common and usually can be found on sale for $3 to $4 per box of 25. Usually around August is the prime time to purchase them. The major stores have them on sale for the hunters. Remember, we have to take advantage of every bargain we can. After acquiring the game loads, I would pick up a minimum of 50 each, 0 or 00 buckshot. These are sold in packages of 5ea. And usually cost around $3.00 ea. Now that you have the shotgun and the ammunition, its range time. If you have never been to a gun safety class, there are many like the state sponsored "Hunter Safety Course" which can familiarize you with the hunting laws and the safety of the weapon. After taking a safety course, try and find a place out in the country and someone who has experience with shotguns and go have some fun. This is where you can learn the capabilities of your new purchase. You can see what coverage the shotgun has at different distances. You will be amazed at the devastating and rather large ragged hole that is produced with bird shot at close range. Always practice safety.

After acquiring the shotgun, and learning to use it, the next thing I would purchase is the magazine tube extension. Choate™ makes a very good one and it can be purchased for around $30 to $40 dollars.

Second Weapon

After the shotgun, I would start to look for a .22 rifle. I, like many others grew up shooting .22s. I remember being able to buy a box of Winchester Wildcats™ for fifty cents and go out on a Saturday afternoon and shoot cans. That was cheap entertainment but it also provided the fundamentals of shooting. All the time I was

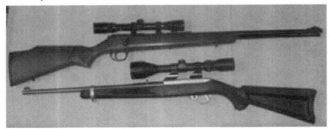

acquiring targets, controlling my breathing, controlling my trigger pull, etc, I thought I was having fun. One of the best games my boys and I would play when they were younger was we would set up ten soda cans on a board at 25 yards, then I would start on one side of the line shooting with a .22 pistol, they would start on the other end and we would race to see who would get the most cans down. In the beginning, I would usually be on can 6 before they caught me. After a few thousand rounds, the boys were starting to wear me out. The point of this story is that the .22 rifle is a cheap way of improving your shooting skills and having fun at the same time. I would suggest looking for a magazine fed rifle like the Ruger 10/22™. It is an excellent rifle, fairly accurate out of the box, and has a multitude of accessories that can be added to it to increase its accuracy and firepower. Look for them used in the classified or pawn shops. They are also carried new at the discount stores. New they average around $250 but they can be found for around $100 used. Ammunition is relatively inexpensive still. You can buy a brick, which is the term for 500 rounds, for around $15. Try different types and manufacturers of ammunition in your rifle. I have seen the POA, point of aim, change by over 2 inches between manufacturers. Once you figure out which brand shoots the best in your rifle, buy at least 3 or 4 bricks and keep them stored. The .22 can be used for taking small game and even large game in an emergency.

Third Weapon

My advice for your next purchase would be a handgun for self defense. The pros of handguns are that they are compact, concealable, and in the right hands are very lethal. Many have a misconceived notion that handguns are evil. A general fact of life is that any inanimate object can be neither evil nor good by itself. It is all how it is used. I know that there are several accidents, some of them fatal, within homes that have handguns. But, just like a knife in the kitchen or prescription drugs in the cabinet, if children are allowed access to them there will also be accidents. The number one home accident is drowning. Even though drowning is the number one accident in the home, we have not tried to pass legislation against bathtubs and swimming pools. Yet we are constantly bombarded with legislation to ban handguns. Needless to say, the biggest con of handguns is the users. Now that we have discussed the philosophy of handguns lets take a look at the different types. The main ones we will be discussing for self-defense are revolvers and semi-automatics.

There are two different types of revolvers. The oldest variety is the single action. The single-actions are the pistols that you see on the westerns where the cowboy has to cock the hammer back in order to fire. I cut my teeth on a Ruger Bearcat™ .22 single action revolver. I guess about the age of 7 or 8, I began to shoot my dad's. I still have it and it is probably one of my favorites. My other

favorite single-action is my Ruger Super Blackhawk™ 44 magnum. With 240 grain Hornady XTP hollow points, it is a deer-killing machine. The pros of the single-action are that they

are very stout, very reliable, and fairly safe. The cons of the single-actions are their slow reload rate, and the disadvantage of having to cock the hammer with every shot. Now I know that there are some real Jesse James or Billy the Kid types out there that say they can be just as proficient as anyone with a double action. I am not going to doubt their ability, but again their ability has come from many hours on the range. The single action revolver was a good choice for the late 1800s to protect yourself with, but if it was still viable why don't we see the police and military issuing them? The single action revolvers are a tool for a certain job, but I do not consider a single action revolver a good choice for a self-defense handgun.

The double action revolver is probably the most popular handgun model ever sold. Everyone from Colt to Ruger to Taurus has manufactured them for over 100 years. The majority of police departments have just recently discontinued using them en lieu of

the semiautomatics. The double action revolvers are very dependable, are manufactured in a variety of calibers, and widely available. The Smith and Wesson .38 revolver up until recently had been the

workhorse of the police for years. Most double action revolvers can be fired either single action, where the hammer is cocked back manually, and in double action mode. Double action mode is when the trigger is pulled the hammer is cocked mechanically and then falls. Due to the hammer being cocked mechanically, the length of the trigger pull is sub-sequentially longer thus making the double action mode harder to shoot accurately comparatively to a single action.

There are many double actions on the market. If you prefer a double action revolver, there are many reliable models on the market. Used Smith and Wesson Model 10 and 15s can be found for around $150 in fairly decent shape. A 4" barrel is a good common size. It isn't as concealable as a 2" snub nose or as protruding as a 6" hunter model. Calibers range from .22 to the monster 500 S&W Magnum. The .22 doesn't make a logical choice for self defense and the 500 is like I said before a monster, more suited for hunting then defense. I would suggest sticking to a 38 or a 357 magnum. I prefer the 357 magnum due to it being able to fire both the 38 and 357 cartridges. The 357 with a standard 158-grain Jacket hollow point is a good defense round.

Once you have purchased your pistol, I would suggest a minimum of 500 rounds of ammunition. I practice with the same ammunition that I carry. Then purchase at least 4 speed-loaders. The old movies always depict the cop pulling individual rounds out of their coat pocket loading their revolvers; this is not what you want to do in a defense situation. I was amazed watching Jerry Miculik shooting 12 rounds in 4.45 seconds. This goes to show that with practice a double action revolver is something to contend with.

The next type of pistol we will discuss is the semiautomatic.

 Notice that it is a semiautomatic not an automatic. The uneducated and the press sometimes one in the same refers to semiautomatic pistols as automatics. A semiautomatic weapon fires one round per trigger pull. The "automatic" fires multiple rounds per trigger pull. The "automatic" is not legal to own for most private citizens. We will be discussing the semiautomatic version. The cartridges for a semiautomatic pistol are loaded into a magazine, which is then inserted into the grip. The slide is then pulled back thus freeing a cartridge from the magazine and as the slide is slid forward, the cartridge is loaded into the chamber. The weapon is now ready to fire.

There are many variations of the semiautomatic pistol. Up until 1971, the most common semiautomatic in the United States was based on John Browning's design. Many know it by the generic name of "Colt 45". We all saw the soldiers in the World War II movies with the famous 1911 in their hand. I thought it was almost nostalgic when I was in the service in the 1980's and we were still shooting 1940s models of the 1911A1. I believe Remington Rand manufactured the one I was shooting. The 1911A1 is an excellent weapon but it does take training, as all weapons do, to be safe and accurate. In 1971, Smith and Wesson introduce the Model 59, which was a safe double-action, high capacity semiautomatic.

Since then, there has been a proliferation of the market with semiautomatics. The most notable would be the Glock. I feel that Glock changed the playing field when they were introduced in the 1980s. I still remember the bad press the pistol received about how it was made of plastic and could get through metal detectors. Again this was another case of the uneducated speaking again. The Glock is a polymer/steel design, making it susceptible to being detected by metal detectors. At first I didn't think much of a "plastic" pistol, after shooting one for the first time in 1987, I had to have one. Since then, I have come to admire and respect the Glock in all shades of caliber and size. The advantages of the Glock are that it has less moving parts than most automatics making it less likely to malfunction. The disadvantage of the Glock is that it has only one safety, which is located on the trigger. If there is a round in the chamber and the trigger is pulled, it will fire. I am not trying to offend any of the other manufacturers and their fans, I have owned a multitude of brands and models, we have standardized with the Glock.

The caliber and size will be a personal preference. I began carrying Glocks in 9mm but since being enlightened by one of my brothers in Iraq, I began carrying 40 S&W or 45 ACP. Reason being, 9mm doesn't have the knockdown of energy that the others have. The drawback from the smaller to the larger caliber is the recoil. Basically, the 40 S&W kicks a little harder than the 9mm, and the 45 kicks a little harder than the 40 S&W. I feel that the 40 S&W is a good midrange cartridge for knockdown power and recoil. We use both the full size Model 22, and the Model 23 compact model.

Due to all the different cartridges and models available, I have condensed ours down to the Model 22 and 23. The cartridges are the same, and the magazine of the Model 22 fits the Model 23. The old adage of KISS, keep it simple stupid works here too.

Due to the changing of the guard at the White House, and the general distaste of handguns by Congress, the prices of Glocks and other high capacity pistols are in a steady upwards sweep. In 2007, you could have bought a police trade-in Glock Model 22 for around $300 and the magazines could be purchased for $10 ea used. Currently, December of 2008, I haven't seen many pistols for sale, and the used magazine supply has all but dried up. New magazines can still be purchased for approximately $25 ea. That is up by $10 from last year, but still a good buy.

If you can find a decent Glock from around $400 to $500, I would buy it. Remember that you could possibly be protecting yourself and your family with this weapon, so don't think cheap. Get the best that you can afford. After the weapon, you need to acquire a minimum of 4 magazines per pistol. That will give you 60 rounds of firepower loaded and ready to go.

Once you have acquired the weapon, next I would purchase a minimum of 1000 rounds. This will cost you another $280 dollars. I say 1000 rounds because at least 500 rounds should be used in practice, the other 500 rounds should be on hand anytime.

Fourth Weapon

The last acquisition should be a centerfire rifle. Just like the shotguns and the handguns there are a multitude of models, brands and calibers. Over the years I have acquired everything from single-shots, bolt-actions, lever-actions, and semiautomatics. The main use in a survival situation would be for big game hunting and possibly self-defense. Just like the handguns, each has its limitations and capabilities. The single-shots now come in a variety of calibers and have the capability of changing out from shotgun to rifle. They are relatively inexpensive. I have seen them for sale around the $200 price range new and as little as $75 used. They are very dependable.

The next style would be the bolt-action. Most bolt actions are based on the German Mauser design. The Mauser design has been around since 1871. It is a proven design and very reliable. It comes in a variety of calibers and brands. I have a Spanish Mauser that was converted to .308 Winchester that was made in 1916 and is still shooting today. Another favorite of mine is the British Enfield chambered in .303. Both of these rifles were battle proven all over the world. One account during WWII was that a platoon of British soldiers armed with Enfields drove the Germans off. Later accounts by German soldiers were that the British were firing so fast that they thought they were coming up against a couple of machinegun nests. The .303s can still be found in fair shape around the $200 price range. Whatever the bolt gun you pick, try to find one in a standard caliber like .308, 30.06, or even the .270. The reasons being, would be the availability of cartridges. I own several different magnum rifles that I use for deer hunting, but the availability of the rounds is slim. A good time to find a bolt-action rifle is right after hunting season ends. Many sell their rifles and most have scopes on them. Check the classified ads and sometimes you can find bargains on internet sites like Craigslist.

The lever-action is the next style to be considered. This rifle type has probably killed more deer than any other type. I killed my first deer with a Marlin 336C in 30-30. The lever-actions are also very reliable and dependable. They come in a multitude of calibers and brands. A good combination would be a lever-action rifle in the matching caliber of your pistol. There are several lever-actions made in .357 Magnum. Lever-actions can be found at a lot of the discount stores like Wal-Mart rather inexpensively. Also, like the bolt-actions, check after the hunting season in the classifieds and at pawnshops. I have seen good rifles in the .30-30 caliber and .35 Remington sell for under $200.

The last group of center-fire rifles we will take a look at are the semiautomatics. Many of the major manufacturers like Remington and Browning make semiautomatics for hunting. The style we will be looking at will be considered paramilitary type. These would include the SKS, AK47, AR15, and the HK.

The SKS has an integral or built-in 10-round magazine and is chambered in the soviet round of 7.62 x 39. The ballistics of this round is similar to the .30-30. It was so heavily imported that at one time it was replacing the 30-30 as a favorite deer rifle. There are many after market products made for the SKS to include sporterized stocks and scope mounts. The SKS at one time could be bought for under $100. A good SKS can still be purchased around the $200 to $300 range.

The next semiautomatic rifle is the AK47. The AK47 replaced the SKS as the primary weapon of the Soviet Bloc countries. It was cheap to manufacture, simple design and utilized the same round as the SKS, the 7.62x39. A removable 30-round magazine feeds it. The AK47 became infamous during the Vietnam War. The design was so forgiving that it has been said it could be thrown into a mud hole, washed off and fired. It is a good weapon but currently it is getting more expensive by the hour it seems. The rifle can be found around the $400 to $500 range with the magazines in the $15 range.

The AR15 is the commercial model of the military M16. It is a semiautomatic, gas-operated, magazine-fed, chambered in 5.56mm. It can be found in several different platforms from a carbine model, M4, which has a collapsible stock and 16-inch barrel to a target model with a 20-inch bull barrel. The AR15 platform is my personal choice. I use a M4 with a holographic site for coyote hunting and a DPMS Panther chambered in .308 for deer hunting. The AR15 in 5.56 is very light on the recoil and a joy

to shoot. The M4 variety lends itself well to people with a smaller frame due to the collapsible stock, which can be adjusted for the shooter. Again, like any of the "assault rifles" the prices on these are going up fast. They can be found in the $800 to $1000 range and the magazines can still be found new for around $15. The .308 versions are a little more expensive with the rifles going for about $1400 and the magazines around $50.

The HK-91 is another semiautomatic made by Heckler & Koch and it is chambered in 7.62 NATO cartridge. The HKs have just about dried up on the market today. There are some new ones being manufactured here in the United States under the model PTR 91. It is an American HK91. It is a precision made weapon capable of bringing down deer at 500yds. and better. It is rather pricey though. I haven't seen any sell under $1000 in a year or two. The magazines can be found used relatively cheap. I purchased 100 of them in 2007 for a dollar a piece. I had to cull about 15 out of the bunch, but the others work flawlessly. I saw the same magazines for sell just last month for three dollars each.

Try and purchase at least 10 magazines for your rifle and try and keep at least 500 rounds in stock for your rifle. I would suggest buying 1000 rounds at a time. In 5.56 or 7.62x39, it would cost about $450 per thousand. Keep 500 in stock, practice with the other.

In Conclusion

I know we covered a lot of ground in a relatively small space, but the main thing is that it is our responsibility as Christians to protect ourselves. Whether you buy a 12ga single-shot shotgun or a tricked out AR15, first get very familiar with it. The only way you can become familiar with it is practice, practice, and practice. And I can never stress this enough, BE SAFE!

9

Just the Beginning

This book is by no means conclusive of all the things that are needed for each individual or family. I have tried to cover the major items and how to acquire them. There is one thing that you can't buy that is the most important item you can obtain is the right attitude. I call it a Joseph attitude. We can take so many examples from his life to use in ours. The one lesson that always comes to mind is in Genesis chapter 50.

[20]But as for you, ye thought evil against me; but God meant it unto good, to bring to pass, as it is this day, to save much people alive.

Genesis 50:20 (KJV)

If you remember the story, Joseph is speaking to his brothers after the death of their father. The brothers feared retribution from Joseph now that Jacob had died. But, unlike his brothers and also unlike most of us today, Joseph saw the bigger plan. Joseph saw God in everything he did and everything that happened to him. I fully believe that Joseph didn't blame God for circumstances but thanked Him. Oh, that we would thank God for the bad times as well as the good times. We are on the start of an economic depression in America right now. If you are a blood-washed brother or sister with me in Christ, then you know that God has never said OOPS. Have we not as Americans strayed from God? Is it not proof in point what we have elected into our representative offices that we no longer care about God? God has not been surprised by the economy of America. He also has not been taken back by the possibly of the loss of your job.

Not only has God not been surprised but also He has told us throughout His Word that the times were coming and be ready. So, how can we have an attitude like Joseph?

First off, get off your pity pot. Every time Joseph was knocked down, he got back up, dusted himself off and went at it full steam ahead. If he had been a typical Christian today, he would have never made it past being a slave at Potiphar's house. He would have been taking sick days and going to the doctor and getting anti-depressant pills to deal with reality. Folks, I know of what I speak. I have been knocked down numerous times, and have had mild depression for at least an hour. But, just like Joseph, we have to look at our situation and remember GOD IS IN CONTROL. Unlike Congress, who tells us that they knew better than us? God does know better for you. We just don't see the "Big Picture" all the time. Second, grow where you are planted. As with Joseph, we should accept our situation for the good and do the best we possibly can with what we have. Erma Bombeck may have coined, "When you have lemons, make lemonade." but Joseph lived it. He was sold into slavery by family, moved up to manager, back down to prisoner, then became a manager of the prison, then placed as the number two man in the strongest country in the world at the time. He made the best of what he had. What did he have you may ask? He had faith that God was with him, no matter what.

Take a cue from Joseph, and do the best with what you have. Thank God for the job you have if you have one. If unemployed, reassess your situation and remember God knows.

Christian Preparedness is 90% attitude, 10% possessions. Without a Joseph attitude, during hard-times the only thing I can tell you to store up would be anti-depressants. With a Joseph attitude, that rice and beans just became a feast that supplied you and your family with the nourishment needed. Thank God for Him telling you to get ready. Because, as my Lord said,

[20] **Remember the word that I said to you, 'A servant is not greater than his master.' If they persecuted Me, they will also persecute you. If they kept My word, they will keep yours also.** [21] **But all these things they will do to you for My name's sake, because they do not know Him who sent Me.**

John 15:20-21 (NKJV)

Made in the USA
Lexington, KY
02 July 2011